Just My Reflection . . .

Just My Reflection . . .

Helping Parents to Do Things Their Way
When Their Child Dies

Frances Dominica ASSP

To dear Mary and Brian –
    Thank you for Peter and
for all that you and he and
his brothers have given us and
taught us –
        With very much love –
April 1997.   Frances.

DARTON·LONGMAN+TODD

First published in 1997 by
Darton, Longman and Todd Ltd
1 Spencer Court
140–142 Wandsworth High Street
London SW18 4JJ

ISBN 0–232–52211–1

Phototypeset by Intype London Ltd
Printed and bound in Great Britain by
Page Bros, Norwich

My body is just my reflection . . .
When you die you leave your reflection.
Your real self leaves your body and
goes into another world . . . where
it will be the happiest life of all . . .
God has the answers, we have the
questions, and only in the end
will he tell us the answers.
God has kept that new life a secret
and I am glad because it will give
us a surprise, it will give us such
a big surprise.

Garvan Byrne, aged 11, a year before he died.

For Estelle, Anwar and Sharee
and in memory of
Frances
1921–1925,
my mother's beloved little sister,
after whom I was named.

This book is written in the hope that it may be useful as a handbook for easy reference at the time of the death of a child.

It is written for the friend, the pastor, the nurse, the doctor, the funeral director or anyone else who may find him- or herself beside the family at such a time. Most of all it is written for members of the child's family in the belief that, if things are to be done well, then they must be done their way.

Acknowledgements

Many people have helped me in the preparation of this book. In particular I would like to thank parents of children who have died, friends and professional colleagues who have so generously given me the benefits of their wisdom gained through experience.

I thank the Helen House team, in whose wonderful companionship I have delighted over the years, sharing laughter and tears, vision and learning; my special thanks are due to Mrs Bronwen Bennett for her help in assembling the second half of the book and to the Reverend Michael Smith for composing two prayers for inclusion.

I am very grateful to Jacki and David Morris for allowing me to reproduce the service sheet used at Ben's funeral; also to Kim Beechey's parents, Diane and Colin, and to her friends for agreeing to let me publish their letters written to her after her death.

Professor David Baum, paediatrician and friend of children, has been and is a source of incalculable encouragement.

My Sisters in the Society of All Saints have lovingly supported me in this venture, as in so many before. Most of all I am deeply grateful to Sister Beverly Ruth who has not only typed the manuscript but has greatly enriched it through her knowledge, enthusiasm and sensitivity.

Frances Dominica ASSP, RGN, RSCN, FRCN

Contents

Non-Christian customs surrounding death

The Funeral Service and Afterwards

What Friends Can Do

PART TWO

APPENDICES AND REFERENCES

EXAMPLE OF A SERVICE SHEET

Foreword

No book can turn the clock back: no text can mend the torn heart of parents whose child has died. However the gentle and wise words of Frances Dominica contained in this small volume offer a framework of support which at least may replace some of the salt to the wounds with balm in the practical management of the hours and days following a child's death.

This book is in some ways a companion to Helen House which Frances Dominica established as a source of practical help to children with terminal and life-threatening conditions and their families. The hallmarks are sensitivity without an excess of sentiment, practicality based on experience, and the good judgement and touch of a professional who knows that the present must be catered for but in such a way that the best interests of the surviving family are also served for the years and decades that follow.

J. D. Baum MA, MSc, MD, FRCP
President of the Royal College of Paediatrics and Child Health
1997–2000

Introduction

To live through the death of your child is perhaps one of the most painful experiences known to humankind. It is instinctive in parents to nourish and protect their child. Death is to be fought, even to the point of sacrificing your own life, but sometimes the fight is lost. Life is quite literally beyond control. The death of your child leaves you feeling helpless, guilty, powerless and broken.

Nothing can take away the pain you experience, but there are small ways in which it can be made a little less appalling. If you feel that you have some control, not over the fact of death itself — would that it could be so! — but over the events, encounters and exchanges surrounding death, then maybe you can find a little comfort in the midst of the hell of it all. This book is written in the hope that even just a few parents will be given back the control which is theirs by right. If the words which follow are helpful then it is thanks to parents and families who have themselves lived through the dying and death of their beloved child and who, in their generosity, have taught us what is helpful and what is unhelpful. They are the true experts and it is from them we learn. When those of us who are alongside them feel that we know it all and that they have nothing more to teach us, then it is time we moved on and focused our attention elsewhere.

Helen House opened in 1982 offering friendship and practical support to children with life-limiting illness and to their families. Soon afterwards we began to put together a loose-leaf file of songs, hymns, readings, poems and prayers suitable for use at a child's funeral. Many are well known, others less so; often new ones are brought to our attention by families themselves. Gradually we have come to realise how vital it is to offer the family of a child who has died the opportunity to create the funeral service themselves. It is their final act of caring for their child and it can never be repeated or improved upon. It is therefore vital that it is as perfect for them as may be if memories of the occasion are to comfort rather than disappoint. Only they can know exactly what is most appropriate. 'Does it sound awful to say I enjoyed it?' a young mother asked me as we stood outside the crematorium chapel after the funeral of her son on what would have been his second birthday. 'It was just right for him.' Of course it was right. In the days after his death she and her husband had put the service together with a love and sensitivity and an inner knowledge which no one else could emulate.

To help families to do this we often lend them the loose-leaf file because so many have said they found it useful. We decided to make it more widely available, and this forms the second half of this book. The first half consists of a number of other ways in which we have learnt to do all we can to give control into the hands of the true experts, the families themselves.

I have come to believe that there is in every human being the instinct to meet death with a nobility and a 'rightness' which we rarely know we possess ahead of time. It is an instinct at gut level, deeper far than reason or rationale. The more developed and sophisticated and cerebral the society in which we live, the deeper that instinct tends to be buried. But it is there. Those of us who find ourselves alongside those who grieve the death of a child need to have an unfaltering belief in that inherent instinct. The families are the experts, but they need others to affirm them. Those others are not there to tell them how they should think or behave, but to stay with them while they discover the answers within themselves.

The word 'companion' has come to have great meaning for me in recent years. Its derivation is *cum + panis*, to share bread. Bread is symbolic of that which we need for survival and nourishment. Bread is a very basic food; it is not fussy or sophisticated. In the presence of very great suffering we feel helpless and inadequate. We need to remember that in living through the death of a child what a family needs most is basic friendship. The most valuable thing we have to offer is companionship, companionship in which we are unashamedly ourselves and in which we make it feel safe for the one we accompany to be him- or herself.

Before Helen House opened I met a little girl who had cancer. She and her mother and her brother lived in a small flat in our town and I got to know them well in the last six months of the child's life. Her mother determined that she would care for her daughter in her own home, once it was recognised that she would not recover. I lived with them during the last few days of the little girl's life and through the days which followed until the funeral. The mother, who was Irish, had not lost touch with her instinct to do things the way she knew was right. I stayed with her and marvelled. I learned more in those few days than I had throughout my nursing career.

No doctor, nurse, pastor or funeral director was going to deter this woman from keeping her child's body at home in her bedroom until the funeral. It was she who washed and dressed the little one after death, she who brushed her hair and arranged toys and flowers around her and went in and out of the room so naturally in the days which followed. It was the mother who lifted her daughter's body into the coffin on the day of the funeral and ensured that everything was as it should be for the next stage in the child's journey. In a devastatingly imperfect world everything was as perfect as it could be.

It is to that mother, Estelle, and her two children, Anwar and Sharee, and to all the families I have come to know since then whose beloved children have died, or may soon die, that this book is dedicated. If it helps others in their own tragedy, then our thanks are due to the children and families who alone can say, 'I know how you feel.'

Part One

The Death of a Child

The circumstances of death

The death of a child in this country is rare, yet for approximately 10,000 families in England and Wales each year statistics are irrelevant. The thing every parent dreads most happens. Their child dies.

Children die in very different circumstances. Many die in early infancy. At two extremes, some die instantaneously, others live for many years with a progressive illness. In the case of sudden death there is no opportunity for preparation or anticipatory grieving. With illness or handicap which is compatible with life for a period of time the family will experience bereavement long before their child dies. They may want to make plans for the time of their child's death while the child is still alive, or they may feel unable or unwilling to do so. We need to remember that no two situations are ever the same.

Many families, given the choice and the necessary support, choose to care for their child at home. Every effort should be made to make this possible. In any case what matters most is that the child and the family feel 'at home' wherever they are.

Towards the time of death

The most important people in a child's life, usually the parents, brothers and sisters, should, where at all possible, be with their child when he or she is dying, whether at home, in hospital, hospice or elsewhere.

To be in bed with the child, sharing a sofa or a large enough, comfortable armchair, may be best, given the choice.

If the child is still conscious, he or she may still have questions to ask and hopes or fears to express. These need to be met with honesty and simplicity and the reassurance that they are being heard.

It is natural to cuddle a child, to stroke the child gently, to talk to him or her. It is important to remember that hearing is usually one of the last faculties to be lost and that just because the child is no longer able to respond, it does not mean to say that he or she cannot hear.

The professional person's task at this stage, or that of the caring friend, is to ensure that the child is as comfortable as possible and is suffering the minimum of distress, all the while giving gentle reassurance that there is no need to be afraid.

The use of prescribed drugs will often be helpful in relieving distressing symptoms but sometimes the family may ask for a drug to be withheld, for example, 'so that his eyes are still open when his grandparents come to say goodbye'. The parent's wishes should normally be granted, even if it could be argued that this causes the child unnecessary distress. The parents may survive for many years and they may have greater peace of mind if they feel that they had some control, even at this last stage of their child's life. They may in any case need to talk about their apprehension concerning the effect of a particular kind of medication before they can consent to its use.

Sisters and brothers at the time of death

It has been our experience that it is best for sisters and brothers to be closely involved at this stage, as at all other stages, whatever their age or understanding. To be excluded may lead to deep-seated distress and anger for years to come.

Including them means answering questions honestly, asking them their wishes and their views and explaining things in a simple, straightforward way.

We may instinctively try to protect children from such pain, but to exclude them from the death of their sister or brother may give rise to fantasies more terrible than reality. Reality can more often be contained and controlled in the memory. Fantasy readily runs out of control.

Ideally the room where the sick child is being cared for should be arranged to allow other children to come and go freely. Someone should have the job of taking care of their immediate needs and focusing attention on them. These needs may be very great in the hours following the death of their brother or sister. They may feel an urgent need to protect themselves or to be protected in their extreme vulnerability.

However strongly *we* may feel about the benefits of including well children at every stage, once we have offered the view and given support for their inclusion, the parents must feel free to make their own decision. They usually know their children better than anyone else.

Grandparents, relatives and friends

The grandparents' position is very painful. Not only are they watching their grandchild die, but they are also having to stand by and see the extreme distress of their own child. Their presence and practical role at this stage can only be decided with the parents.

Other relatives and close friends may or may not be welcome when the child is dying.

A time like this often brings the best out of human relationships but it can also bring out the worst. It needs great skill to deal with arguments and dissension in such a setting. It is not for the friend or professional to take sides but to try to ensure the greatest comfort and well-being of the sick child.

The trusted friend or professional person may well need to protect the child's family when relatives or friends try to make decisions on behalf of the family. This attempt to take over is often made with the best motives and with a genuine desire to help the family but it may be unhelpful. Given time and support parents will make their own decisions. Meanwhile it may be that the friend or professional can offer the greatest help by giving time to relatives and friends, so taking some of the pressure away from the family.

When a child dies – the death having been expected

The parents will often ask if the child has died. Their next question will be 'What do we have to do?' *There is no hurry to do anything.*

Those closest to the child may want time just to be there with the child. They may want to pray or they may ask someone else to pray with them for their child, either formally or informally. For some parents this may be the moment when they say 'Goodbye' to their child.

When the parents are ready they may choose to do the various things necessary for their child themselves, with or without help, or they may ask someone else to do these things for them.

The child may be washed. Nails may need attention. Wounds may be re-dressed, using waterproof dressings. It may sometimes seem advisable to introduce cotton wool into the anus but other orifices do not normally need packing.

The child is dressed in whatever clothes the parents choose (nightdress or pyjamas, favourite track suit, first Communion dress, Batman outfit, shroud – nothing is inappropriate if it is the choice of the family). The child's hair is brushed or combed in the usual style, and the body gently straightened on the bed.

It may be helpful to place a small cushion or pillow under the child's chin for two or three hours to ensure that the jaw does not fall open. Likewise the eyelids may be gently closed and pads of wet cotton wool may be placed on them for a time. If there is any problem with this the funeral director will be able to help.

When the death of a child is sudden and unexpected

When a child dies suddenly and unexpectedly the coroner is informed, normally by the doctor. A coroner's officer (who may be police or civilian) will follow up enquiries. If police visit the child's home they will normally be in an unmarked car and where possible in civilian clothes. The child's body will normally be taken with the minimum of delay to a hospital mortuary by a funeral director acting under instructions from the coroner's office. A post-mortem may follow.

The lack of time and opportunity for the family to say goodbye to their child or to do anything for their child at this stage can be extremely distressing.

Once the coroner is satisfied and the body is released it may continue to be cared for in the hospital mortuary, or may be taken home or to the chapel of rest belonging to a funeral director.

After the Death

The place where the child's body will lie until the funeral

The choices listed below assume that the coroner is not involved or that he has been involved but has subsequently released the body.
When a child dies at home the parents may choose:

— to continue to care for their child's body at home for some or all of the days leading up to the funeral;
— to have their child's body taken to a chapel of rest belonging to funeral director;
— to use the 'little room'/'special room' of a children's hospice, if this is available.

When a child dies in hospital the parents may choose:

— to use the hospital mortuary (and viewing room when required);
— to use any of the places mentioned above.

When a child dies in a children's hospice the parents may choose:

— to use the 'little room'/'special room', furnished with a bed or cot, comfortable chairs and anything else the family may choose. Its design will be like that of an ordinary room but it will have a built-in cooling system, sufficient to allow the child's body to remain there for several days, regardless of outside temperatures;
— to take the child home;
— to use a chapel of rest.

When a child dies at school or in any other place, whether from illness or accident, after the initial necessary action is taken and legal requirements are met, the parents should still be given the choice of where their child's body will be cared for until the funeral.

Caring for the child's body at home

Many people do not realise that parents have an absolute right to care for their child's body at home unless the death has been reported to the coroner, and even then it may be possible once the coroner has released the body.

A child who dies in hospital or anywhere else other than home and who is small enough can simply be wrapped in a blanket and carried to a car and so transported home. A funeral director will give the necessary help for a child who cannot be transported in this way.

Hospital staff and others should co-operate fully in implementing the parents' choice.

Parents may like to wait until they reach home before washing and dressing their child.

In preparing the bed which is to be used it may be helpful to place waterproof protection over the mattress. The bed may be in the child's bedroom or any other suitable room.

Family members may want to arrange flowers, toys, photographs and candles, and anything else to make the room special for the child.

They may want to remove equipment which the child has needed and which is no longer necessary, but they may not yet be ready to do this.

The room needs to be kept as cool as possible, with fresh air circulating freely. This will help to delay the changes in the body which sometimes give off an unpleasant smell. Air fresheners may help.

Once relatives and friends have overcome their initial apprehension, usually due to unfamiliarity with death at home, they may well find that some of their fears are overcome by seeing and even touching the body of the child, in the more natural environment of home as opposed to hospital or chapel of rest.

In hot weather or in circumstances where it is difficult to keep the room sufficiently cool it may be best for the child's body to be taken to a chapel of rest after two or three days, but this is not always necessary. It may sometimes be possible to borrow a cooling machine. Embalming the child is another option and this is best done at the funeral director's premises.

The child's family will often find themselves in the unexpected role of comforter to those who come to visit in the days following their child's death. If the family has been allowed to be in control of events surrounding the death and to grieve in their own way, supported by those around them, they will be more able to meet the shock and raw grief of others.

Sisters and brothers seeing the body of the child who has died

Children of all ages often have frightening and lurid ideas of what people look like when they have died, for example, lots of blood, the body decapitated or squashed, the flesh turned black. These ideas often originate from films, videos or comics.

Children may also wonder how you know for sure that someone is dead. Older children may be reluctant to admit that they do not know the answers to their own questions. It is almost always helpful for them to see their sister or brother after the death, whether they have been present at the time or not. They will need to know that when someone dies their body temperature gradually drops until eventually they feel very cold to touch.

They may ask many questions to which we do not have the answers but, if they see their sister or brother for themselves, at least some of their fears may be dispelled. Some may find the analogy of the butterfly emerging and leaving its chrysalis behind helpful. Others may like to think of the body as a shell.

If the child's body is badly mutilated it may still be possible for sisters or brothers to see some part of the body, for example, a hand or foot, or the face, while the rest of the body is covered. Children – and adults – find it harder to believe that someone has really died if they never see the body. However, the fact that part of the body remains covered may in itself give rise to uncontrolled fantasy and fear. Nothing is perfect in such traumatic situations and one can only do what one believes to be right at the time.

If the brother or sister does not see the body, it may be important to encourage them to talk about it at a later stage. Drawing or playing may be useful ways of working out a way of living with the reality of what has happened.

Telling relatives and friends of the death of a child

Parents will often want to tell relatives and close friends of the death of their child themselves, either in person, or by telephone or letter.

Word of such a tragedy spreads fast, but one way in which friends may be able to help is to offer to inform specific people.

The family may welcome the offer of a friend to spend time with them in the early days of bereavement with the intention of protecting them when they do not feel able to answer the door to visitors or to cope with telephone calls. This is a very personal thing and can only be done with common sense and great sensitivity. The family may be overwhelmed by callers at this stage but would often welcome them in the loneliness of the weeks and months to come.

Telling children in school

Telling children in school that one of their number has died is a particularly difficult task, requiring great sensitivity on the part of the head-teacher, chaplain, or other members of staff. Honesty, directness and simplicity should be the mark of such an announcement.

It will help the children in their shock and grief if they can see for themselves that the adults around them are experiencing the same emotions. To make brief reference to the death of someone who has been amongst them as one of them, and then to carry on as if nothing has happened, is bewildering to the other children, however young.

It is helpful to be given permission to cry, however young or old you are, and to be assured that tears are, in themselves, healing in the outpouring of emotion. To be told that 'Big boys don't cry' or that 'Nice girls don't get angry' is unhelpful and blatantly untrue.

The same principles apply in telling youth groups and other organisations, to which the child may have belonged.

Children like to know that they can talk privately to a teacher or other adult if and when they need to, without having to display their ignorance or vulnerability to their peers.

Some sort of remembrance event at school, marking and cele-brating the child's life and giving an opportunity to express sorrow and all the conflicting emotions that will arise, may be creative and healing.

Special sensitivity is needed in welcoming back into school the brother or sister of a child who has died. They may appreciate being asked if they mind their brother or sister being talked about and if anything can be done to make this time easier for them. The bereaved child will not 'get over' the death in days or weeks, or even months, and will need great patience and understanding on everyone's part. Grief may manifest itself in many ways, some-times in behaviour which is difficult to accept.

Many families welcome the spontaneous visits of children who have been friends of their child. Their natural way of talking about the child and their feelings is usually comforting. Their honesty is appreciated.

Deaths which are reported to the coroner

These include:

– a child who has not been seen by a doctor in the fourteen days prior to death;
– any sudden or unexpected death;
– death at operation or procedure before full recovery from anaes-thetic;

– death occurring within a year and a day of an accident considered to be the direct cause of death;
– any suspicious circumstances, e.g. violence, neglect, poisoning.

The coroner will decide whether a post-mortem is legally required.

Post-mortem examination

Sometimes a post-mortem is required by law, for example if the child has not been seen by a doctor in the fourteen days prior to death.

The parents' consent is sought in situations where a post-mortem is not obligatory but where it is thought that it would be useful in revealing the effects of the disease on the child, or for other reasons which the doctors concerned will explain to the parents. This decision may be exceedingly difficult to make. The parents may find it a little easier if they know that other children with a similar condition may be helped by the knowledge gained through a post-mortem examination on their child. In some cases, the findings of a post-mortem examination may affect decisions made by the parents about further pregnancies.

Where a choice must be made, those standing by the parents while they reach their decision must be very sensitive and never coercive. The parents may feel that their child's body has already suffered enough trauma and they must not be made to feel guilty if they refuse permission.

Parents can be reassured that if they do decide to give permission for a post-mortem examination it will still be possible for them to see the body of their child afterwards and, possibly, to care for it. It is a surgical operation and is not mutilating; any necessary incisions will have been closed and dressed as in normal surgical procedures. In many cases examination is limited to a specific organ or organs and parents who agree to a post-mortem may ask that it should be limited in this way. Nevertheless some parents may feel emotionally unable to see or touch their child's body after a post-mortem examination and they must be given plenty of time and, where possible, the right environment in which to say their goodbyes before the procedure.

Many parents find that meeting with their doctors to hear the result of the post-mortem, both what was found and what was not, and why the child died, is in the long term a comfort.

At a later stage they may feel the need to discuss the findings again.

Donor organs

Some parents will find it comforting to think that, by allowing a part of their child's body to be used, another child may be given the gift of life and health. They can be assured that the recovery of organs and tissues is carried out with great care by qualified surgeons. The body of their child will not be disfigured.

The use of donor organs does of course depend on those organs being healthy and also, with the exception of the cornea and heart valves, on the donor dying in hospital. The donor must not have malignant disease (with the exception of some cerebral tumours), major sepsis, viral hepatitis or be HIV positive.

Two doctors will carry out a series of tests independently in order to confirm that the child is 'brain stem dead' before any procedure to remove organs can take place. Brain stem death usually follows a severe brain injury which causes all brain stem activity to stop. This may be the result of a major accident or of a clot, haemorrhage or severe swelling causing interruption of blood supply to the brain. It can be very painful for parents to say goodbye to their child while the child is still being ventilated and therefore appears to be 'alive'. They need to know ahead of time that although they may be able to accompany them to theatre, they will not be with them when they are disconnected from the ventilator. To know that someone understands their distress in this respect will help a little.

A booklet entitled *Questions and Straight Answers about Transplants* is published by the United Kingdom Transplant Support Service Authority. It may be obtained by contacting:

Publicity Services Section: UKTSSA
Foxden Road
Stoke Gifford
Bristol BS 12 6RR
Tel: 0117 975 7575

If, for whatever reason, the parents' offer to donate organs from their child is refused, they may feel a sense of hurt and rejection. The reasons for refusal need to be carefully explained and genuine gratitude expressed for the generosity of the parents.

The transplant co-ordinator will always be willing to spend time with the family if requested.

Embalming and the use of cosmetics

Embalming is sometimes useful if the child's body is to remain at home until the funeral, or if there is a longer than usual delay between the time of death and the funeral.

It is a process performed by the funeral director at his premises in which blood in the arteries is replaced by a preservative, normally a solution of formalin. This delays decomposition of the body and the resultant smell.

Cosmetics will not often need to be used for a child though, appropriately and discreetly used, they may sometimes help to lessen the appearance of bruising for example, or to give the lips a more natural appearance. Cosmetics should not normally be used without the express permission of the child's parents.

Preparing for the Funeral

The funeral director

The choice of funeral director is very important. If it is possible to choose one who is sensitive to the particular needs of a family whose child has died, this is of immense help. The funeral director can do much to help or hinder the family in the initial days of their grief following the death of their child.

The funeral director's role is to inform the parents, in a straightforward and uncomplicated way, of the various choices available to them. Many parents will not know that they can shape the funeral service so that it is fitting for their child and family.

The funeral director's advice may be sought, but the family should never feel coerced into making decisions against their will or before they are ready.

The funeral director can make the difference between an appalling experience which does nothing to convey the love and respect felt for the child, and an event which, in all its unspeakable tragedy, can be looked back on as right for this special child.

The family may choose to make most of the arrangements or may ask the funeral director to do so on their behalf. Whatever is decided, the funeral director should give an itemised written estimate of the costs to the family before acting for them. This will include the fees paid on behalf of the family, e.g. crematorium fees, burial fees, doctor's fees for cremation papers, minister's fees etc., as well as professional fees paid to the funeral directors. Occasionally some of these fees may be waived; therefore it is not always possible to give an exact estimate.

Many funeral directors make no charge for the funerals of babies or small children. They will in any case be able to give advice if there are financial difficulties, as will a social worker.

The minister of religion

The degree of involvement of a minister of religion at the time of a child's death will depend on many things, not least:

– any previous relationship with the child or family;
– requirements of the religion to which the family may belong;
– the character of the minister and whether the support he or she offers is perceived by the family to be relevant.

The majority of families living in the United Kingdom will ask for a minister of the appropriate religion to conduct the child's funeral, although this is not essential. (See section on 'The person who will officiate'.) If the family does not know whom to contact, the funeral director will offer to do this on their behalf.

The person who will officiate at the funeral

This may be:

– a minister of religion;
– a member of the family or close friend who is able to conduct a meeting;
– a representative of an appropriate organisation.

If the person officiating has not known the child it is essential for him or her to be told something about the child.

Sometimes a person who has known the child but who is not the officiant may be invited to give the address or homily.

Anyone may be invited to take a particular part in the service, for example to read a chosen passage, to sing, to play a musical instrument or to offer some of the prayers.

Announcement of the death

The funeral director will normally offer to arrange for an announcement of the death of a child to be placed in either national or local newspapers or both, but the family may prefer to do this themselves, or not to make such an announcement at all.

The announcement may be brief and factual with the name and date of death only, or it may include as many details as the parents choose – for example, date of birth, illness or accident, place of death, names of family members, funeral arrangements, 'in memoriam' requests, suitable quotations or messages. There are however restrictions in most national daily newspapers.

If this is to be the chief way of notifying those who wish to attend the funeral, it is helpful to place the notice with the newspaper as soon as conveniently possible. Many details of the arrangements may be omitted in the announcement by simply giving the name and telephone number of the funeral director.

Suggested forms for national and local papers

National

BROWN John Alan, beloved son of Mary and Paul, dear brother of Samantha and Joshua, died peacefully on November 1st at home, aged 11 years. Funeral enquiries: F. H. Bloggs and Son, 3, West Street, Markham, Oxon. Tel 01865 333812

Local

BROWN John Alan, beloved son of Mary and Paul, dear brother of Samantha and Joshua and much loved grandson of Edith, Joe and Jane; died peacefully on November 1st at his home after a courageous and fun-filled life, aged 11 years. Funeral on Thursday November 6th at 3 p.m. at All Saints' Church, Littleham, Oxon., and afterwards at St Edmund's School, Markham. Family flowers only but donations welcomed for The Muscular Dystrophy Group to F. H. Bloggs and Son, Funeral Directors, 3, West Street, Markham, Oxon. OX3 7EW.

'A bright light has gone out of our lives.'

Registering the death

The death of all children (including unborn babies over 24 weeks gestation) must be registered with the Registrar of Births, Deaths and Marriages within five days of death.

Parents may choose to register their child's death themselves. If they do not wish to do so, or are unable, the following people may register the death:

Deaths in houses and public institutions

- a relative of the deceased, present at the death;
- a relative of the deceased, in attendance during the last illness;
- a person present at the death;
- a relative of the deceased, residing or being in the sub-district where the death occurred;
- the person causing disposal of the body;
- the occupier* if he knew of the happening of the death.

Deaths not in houses or dead bodies found

- any relative of the deceased having knowledge of the particulars required to be registered;
- any person present at the death;
- any person who found the body;
- any person in charge of the body;
- the person causing disposal of the body.

The doctor who has seen the child after death will provide a signed medical certificate of cause of death or stillbirth to the informant who will register the death. Legible writing on the part of the doctor may save unnecessary distress when presenting the certificate to the registrar. If the doctor is uncertain as to the cause of death, or has not seen the child in the past fourteen days, or if death occurs within twenty-four hours of surgery or as a result of

* Occupier in relation to a public institution includes the governor, keeper, master, matron, superintendent, or other chief resident officer.

suspicious circumstances, the doctor is not permitted to issue a death certificate but must inform the coroner. The coroner will then make the necessary arrangements to ascertain the cause of death.

The certificate is taken to the registrar's office in the sub-district in which the death took place. The doctor will probably be able to give the necessary information about the place and office hours of the registrar. Alternatively the telephone directory entry is headed Registration of Births, Deaths and Marriages. An appointment is sometimes required, and in any case it is wise to check office hours before setting out.

A simple question and answer interview will take place between the registrar and the person registering the death. Information needed is:

— certificate of the cause of death;
— date and place of death;
— the child's full name, home address, the date and place of birth;
— the parents' full names, home addresses and occupations.

The correct entry is made in the register and signed by the informant and the registrar. Copies of the entry can be obtained for £3.00 (1997 in England and Wales) in the first month, the amount increasing thereafter.

The registrar will supply the certificate of burial or cremation which will be required by the funeral director.

Planning the funeral

Many people think that it is good to 'get the funeral over' as soon as possible.

Some religions and cultures require that the funeral and disposal of the body happens within one or two days of death.

For others, however, it may feel better to allow sufficient time to plan all the details of the funeral without a feeling of hurry. For many families the optimum time for the funeral to take place is about five days after the death of their child.

There is more likelihood that relatives and friends who wish to attend the funeral will be able to do so, given more notice.

The choice of the day and time will partly depend on the availability of the services and amenities which will be needed.

Choosing the coffin

The funeral director will make the parents aware of the range of designs from which they can choose a coffin. White coffins are normally available for children as well as various types of wooden or wood veneer coffins. A wide range of more imaginative and more suitable designs will soon be available. (See Appendix I, Children in Focus.) Parents may choose the lining for the coffin.

A family may make or supply a coffin themselves but it must be strong enough and adequate for the purpose.

Some people may prefer to call the coffin a *casket*, the definition of the word being 'a place for treasure'.

Flowers

The gift of flowers is one way of expressing love and respect for the person who has died and sympathy for the child's family.

Flowers can be bought and then sent by the florist to the funeral director or the child's home, according to the family's wish, with a message and the names of those sending them. Alternatively the person giving the flowers can bring them to the home or to the funeral. The funeral director will normally give the family a list of those who sent flowers and will collect the flower cards for the family if asked to do so.

The family may prefer that only garden or wild flowers are given. Sometimes those who come to the funeral may be invited to bring a single flower and to put it on the coffin or into the grave. On other occasions only the immediate family will give flowers, asking that friends and relatives express their love and sympathy in other ways.

It is not uncommon to see the new grave of a child and the area surrounding it carpeted with gifts of flowers, some of them in the form of elaborate arrangements – a teddy bear, a football or the name of the child for example. If this is comforting for the family then it is entirely good, regardless of the cost.

If a child has died in an accident away from home, families may like to put flowers at the place where their child died, both at the time of death and possibly on the anniversary.

Gifts to charity in memory of a child

Some families will decide to ask relatives and friends to make a gift in memory of the child rather than give flowers at the time of the funeral.

These gifts might be to a favourite charity; to research into the disease which has caused the death of the child; to the place where the child has been cared for; to an organisation or family support group which has meant a lot to the family concerned; or to any other cause which they may choose.

The suggestion that such gifts may be made in memory of the child may be placed in newspaper announcements. The funeral director will also convey this wish to any who enquire. He will, if asked, receive cheques, forwarding the final sum to the appropriate charity.

The funeral director will list those who contribute so that the family may be fully informed.

Specific items in memory of a child

Parents may choose to collect money to buy furniture or equipment for a place or an organisation which has special links with their child.

Gifts towards the planting of a tree or a shrub is another way in which parents may ask others to mark the life and death of their child, living, growing things being symbolic and bringing comfort as time goes by.

An award at school or a trust fund is another way of keeping the memory of their child alive.

Occasionally a charity is set up in memory of the child, but the formalising of such a major project is not often completed at this very early stage of bereavement.

The choice between burial or cremation

For many parents this is an agonizing decision to have to make: to consign the body of their beloved child either to the earth or to flames is too painful even to contemplate.

If burial is being considered, it is important to discover where a plot is available. This may be in ground belonging to a church or in a local authority or privately owned burial ground.

It is possible to arrange for burial to take place on private land, for example in a garden or field, or in woodland, following discussion with local planning authorities. Permission cannot be denied but the exact position may have to be negotiated. Problems can arise if the family subsequently considers moving house.

If cremation is being considered, the superintendent of a crematorium is usually willing to meet members of a newly bereaved family and to answer their questions openly and honestly, often allaying misplaced fears or misconceptions. Families can be assured that the ashes they will be given are the ashes of their child and that they are never mixed with those of anyone else.

Some crematoria do not make any charge in the case of a child under the age of sixteen.

Burial

Those who choose burial often do so because they want to be able to visit the child's grave and to tend it, like a small garden. Some find that the grave becomes a place where they feel particularly close to their son or daughter, and where they can talk to the child. It may be comforting to the family if it is possible for their child to be buried in a family grave, for example with grandparents.

If a child is to be buried the funeral service will normally take place in a church or other building belonging to the relevant faith or in a cemetery chapel, though it can take place in any other appropriate place of the parents' choosing.

Parents may choose whether the burial itself (the interment) is attended by relatives and friends or whether only the immediate family is present, others being invited to remain inside the building until the burial ceremony is complete.

The coffin is usually lowered into the grave by the funeral director and his assistants, but this may be done by members of the family. According to some traditions handfuls of earth may be thrown on to the coffin by some or all present.

The grave will not normally be filled in until family and friends have left but, if they so wish, they may fill in the grave themselves.

The grave may be lined with flowers or with artificial grass ahead of time. Sometimes flowers are thrown on to the coffin after it has been lowered into the ground.

As at all stages, we have come to believe that it is better to include other children in all that is happening. There are many ways of involving them. For example, one imaginative idea is to invite them to set helium balloons free as they stand by the grave, the number of balloons according to the age of the child who has died.

Parents may like to consider reserving a plot next to their child, or buying a family plot.

The headstone

It will probably be some months before a headstone can be placed on the grave so there is plenty of time to choose this and the words which will be inscribed on it.

If the grave is in a churchyard the agreement of the ordained minister acting on behalf of the diocese is needed concerning the choice of material used and the words of the inscription. Similarly, if the grave is in a municipal cemetery the agreement of the appropriate authority must be obtained.

Cremation

If cremation is chosen, a certificate of examination corroborated by two doctors must be completed in addition to the medical certificate of the cause of death. The funeral director will supply a form applying for cremation, to be completed and signed by the next of kin.

The service preceding cremation may take place in the crematorium chapel. Before choosing this option, however, the parents should know that the service cannot normally take longer than thirty minutes, including the time taken for the congregation to enter and leave the chapel. The coffin may be placed in the crematorium chapel before the congregation is invited to enter, or it may be carried in procession with the congregation, or be brought in after the congregation has assembled.

Another option is to hold the main part of the service in a church or other suitable place, using the crematorium chapel only for the brief words of committal. The family may choose for the committal to be private so that only those invited will attend. A further possibility is for the cremation to take place following a brief service of committal in the crematorium chapel attended by the family only or those they may invite; indeed it is possible for the cremation to be private, without family or friends being present. The ashes may then be placed in a casket and taken to a suitable place where a less hurried funeral service can follow. However, this may not be possible until the following day.

It would seem to be helpful in accepting the painful reality of what has happened for the coffin to disappear from sight before the conclusion of the service, but occasionally this is too traumatic for the parents. They may wish to leave the chapel while the coffin is still present and in this, as in all things, their wishes must be respected.

Next of kin, usually only two people, are allowed to be present when the coffin is placed in the cremator. While this is the norm for those who practise Hinduism it is unusual for others.

Small babies are often cremated at the end of the day, allowing the heat of the fire to become less intense.

Ashes

Ashes may be collected from the crematorium by the funeral director or the family, by arrangement, usually at least twenty-four hours after the cremation.

The parents may choose to scatter the ashes in the grounds of the crematorium or in a beautiful place, on the sea, in the hills, or in a place of particular significance for the child. It is important that they stand with the wind behind them when they scatter the ashes.

Another possibility is to bury the ashes. This can be done in the grounds of the crematorium, in a churchyard, or anywhere of the parents' choosing, perhaps in their own garden. It is also possible to bury the ashes in a casket which can be supplied for the purpose by the funeral director. Sometimes the place of burial may be marked by a stone or a plaque, or by a shrub or tree in memory of the child. Families are often invited to plant a rose in the grounds of the crematorium.

Decisions concerning ashes do not need to be made immediately. The crematorium or funeral director will normally agree to take care of them, as will some churches, sometimes for a considerable length of time, before a decision need be reached. Alternatively, the family may take the ashes home in a suitable container supplied by the crematorium or funeral director and make their decision at a later date.

Placing the child in the coffin

The child's body will be placed in the coffin at a time arranged between the parents and the funeral director. The mother and father may wish to lift the child into the coffin themselves, continuing their tending and caring to the very last, but they may prefer that this is done by someone else.

The coffin may be left open until immediately before the funeral or throughout the funeral, or the lid may be fitted at an earlier stage if it seems advisable and if the parents are in full agreement.

Some may like to keep a lock of the child's hair, or a hand-print or foot-print of their child, before the coffin is closed.

If photographs have not already been taken, this is the last opportunity. It may not be the parents' wish to have photographs. Other parents may find it is a long time before they can look at the photographs, or they may choose never to look at them, but if they have been taken, then they have the choice.

Placing things with the child in the coffin

It may be helpful to the family to place favourite toys or possessions treasured by the child in the coffin. A religious symbol, a flower, a photograph or a gift may also seem appropriate.

Thoughts and wishes, words which a mother or father, a brother or sister may have wanted to say but have not been able to until now, a prayer or a poem – these may be placed in the coffin with the child. Sometimes the child's 'best friends' will like to write a letter to place in the coffin. See 'Letters to Kim' in Appendix II.

Some families will not think it helpful or appropriate to do any of these things.

If the child's body is to be cremated there are restrictions as to objects which may remain in the coffin when the lid is fitted. These restrictions normally include metal and man-made fibres. The funeral director will offer advice if asked.

Dressing for the funeral

Culture, social custom or the practice of a particular religion may require that those attending a funeral, or at least the closest rela-tives, will wear distinctive clothing. In Western culture this has traditionally been black. In Eastern practice it is often white.

Many young families will not be expected to conform to a particular way of dressing but have freedom of choice. Some may specifically ask that mourners do not wear black.

All that matters is that the family feels comfortable with their choice. One factor they may well feel is most important is whether their child would have approved of their choice.

Non-Christian Customs Surrounding Death

Families who practise a religion such as Judaism, Islam, Hinduism or Buddhism will normally be well-informed about the rituals surrounding death and the funeral rites approved by the particular faith to which they belong. The following information may be helpful.

Judaism

Strict Orthodox Jews place a feather over the nostrils and the mouth of the dead person for about eight minutes following death.

It is general practice in Judaism for the nearest relative of the same sex as the child to

- gently close the eyes and mouth and place the arms by the side of the body;
- bind the lower jaw;
- remove tubes and instruments;
- place the body on the floor with the feet towards the door;
- wrap the body in a plain white sheet;
- light a candle and place it by the head.

In the absence of a relative anyone may perform these rites but they should wear gloves when handling the child's body. It may be impossible to contact relatives in an Orthodox Jewish family on the Sabbath (sun-down on Friday to sun-down on Saturday).

The body is never left alone. A 'watcher' may stay with the body from the time of death until the burial.

The dead are buried as soon as possible, often on the day of death or within twenty-four hours after death. Orthodox Jews do not permit cremation but progressive Jews sometimes do, as do non-observant Jews.

Embalming is not permitted.

Mourners do not view the body.

Post-mortem examination is forbidden for Orthodox Jews except where required by civil law.

Organ transplant is rarely agreed to, with the exception of the cornea.

The shivah, or seven-day period of formal mourning, follows the burial and the bereaved remain at home and receive visitors. Prayers are said in the home each evening. A central part of the prayers is the recitation of the Kaddish said or sung by the close male relatives. After the period of shivah, Kaddish is said at communal prayers by the male relatives for the period up to stone setting which is eleven months to a year after the funeral.

Islam

The word Islam means submission to the will of God. Its followers are Muslims. The attitude of Muslims towards death is strongly influenced by their belief that suffering and death are part of God's will for them.

The dying child should face Mecca (south-east in the UK). Members of the family may pray at the bedside, whispering into the ear of the child. The child should never be left unclothed as nakedness is deeply shocking to Muslims.

Non-Muslims should not touch the body after death. If it is essential that they do, they should wear disposable gloves. With the family's permission:

– the eyes are closed and the limbs straightened;
– the head is turned towards the right shoulder;
– the body remains unwashed and is wrapped in a plain white sheet.

At death the family will normally perform the necessary rites and recite the prayers. They will:

– close the eyes and straighten the limbs;
– tie the feet together at the big toes;
– bandage the face to keep the mouth closed;
– take the body home or to the mosque for ritual washing;
– place camphor in the armpits and orifices;
– dress the body in white garments.

A woman is forbidden to touch a dead body for forty days after the delivery of her baby.

Post-mortem examinations are accepted where required by civil law. It is important that all the organs removed are returned to the body for burial.

Organ donation is not generally acceptable.

Burial takes place within 24 hours.

UK law requires the use of a coffin which is contrary to Islamic law, and for this and other reasons some families may decide to take their child's body to their country of origin.

Formal mourning continues for one month.

The family remains at home receiving visitors for the first three days.

Hinduism

Hinduism involves the worship of many gods, each one being a manifestation of the Supreme Being.

There are many different practices concerning the rites surrounding death within the Hindu religion.

There is a common belief in reincarnation.

A dying child is often given water from the River Ganges. A thread is sometimes tied around the child's neck or wrist as a sign of blessing and it should not be removed.

Non-Hindus may touch the body after death provided they wear gloves or the body is wrapped in a plain sheet.

There is strong opposition to post-mortem examinations but they are permitted if required by civil law. Organ donation is permitted.

Hindus are normally cremated, but children under the age of

four years are usually buried, as it is believed that they are without sin and will not corrupt the earth. Ideally the cremation or burial takes place on the day of death but this may prove impossible in the United Kingdom. It is important for close relatives to witness the body entering the cremator.

Sikhism

Sikhs believe in reincarnation.

The family is normally responsible for the last offices.

A non-Sikh may close the eyes, straighten the limbs and wrap the body in a plain white sheet.

The family will wash and dress the body.

There are usually no religious objections to post-mortem examination. Organ donation is allowed.

Cremation will take place as quickly as possible, the exception being for an infant dying within a few days of birth, where burial is the norm. The closest relatives may want to be present when the coffin is placed in the cremator, the nearest equivalent to lighting the funeral pyre. The ashes are scattered on a river or in the sea.

The family remains at home receiving visitors for the period of mourning.

Buddhism

Buddhists do not worship a godhead. The Buddha is revered as an example to his followers. The teaching is based on non-violence and compassion for all forms of life. There is great emphasis on spiritual growth.

There is a belief in rebirth, not reincarnation. In each life, learning from past experience, the Buddhist progresses towards the state of perfection known as nirvana. This is a state of mind within the individual rather than a place beyond to be reached. Medication which may make clear thinking difficult is sometimes unacceptable.

There are no special requirements in caring for the body of the child. It is wrapped in a sheet without emblems.

Post-mortem examination is accepted where necessary. Organ donation is not forbidden.

When a child dies special prayers are said for between three and seven days before burial or cremation. Cremation is more usual.

The ceremony is conducted by a relative or by a Buddhist monk (bhikku) or nun (sister). Practices and ritual vary greatly within different Buddhist groups, but there is a universally calm acceptance of death.

The Funeral Service and Afterwards

Suggested structure for a Christian funeral service

The Bidding:
Welcoming those present
Suggesting the reasons for the gathering
  - remembering
  - giving thanks
  - praying for the child and the family
  - saying goodbye
  - grieving

The Word:
From Scripture
From non-scriptural sources – prose, poetry

An Address or Homily

Prayer:
For the child
For those who grieve
In penitence
In thanksgiving
(*This may take the form of a celebration of the Eucharist.*)

The Commendation:
Praying for God's blessing on the child in the life beyond death
Saying goodbye

The Committal:

Lowering the coffin into the grave or moving it towards the cremator.

Psalms, hymns, songs may be chosen and used in any part of the service. Sometimes music is played, either taped or live. It is not wrong to include a child's favourite nursery rhymes or a piece of pop or classical music if this speaks to those present of the child they knew and continue to love.

An alternative style of funeral service

A much less structured form of service may be chosen. An example is the style usually adopted by the Society of Friends (Quakers) in which silence is shared, interspersed with words offered by anyone who feels drawn to speak, read or pray as a tribute or expression of love for the one who has died.

The committal is the only essential part of the funeral rite, anything else being added from choice.

Some families have found it very helpful to be invited by the officiant at the funeral to place things which remind them of their child on a table near the coffin, for example a photograph, a favourite item of clothing, a well-loved toy. Each member of the family may be invited to bring something for the occasion and to take it home with them afterwards.

If the funeral takes place in a church or other suitable place, everyone present may like to light a candle, either during the service or at the end of the service when the coffin has been taken out. This is not normally possible in a crematorium chapel.

The service sheet

The service sheet is not only of practical help to those taking part in the funeral service but is a personal memento for them. It can also be given or sent to those who are unable to be present. There may be a member of the family or a friend who will type the service sheet which can then be photocopied or printed. If not, the funeral director can arrange this.

The cover may have a design, a drawing or photographs on it. As well as the full name of the child (and sometimes the pet name by which he or she has been known), the dates of birth and death are often printed. The family may choose a quotation to be included on the front cover. The words of the service will follow. An invitation to a reception or gathering of friends after the service is sometimes included at the end of the service sheet.

In the same way the family may choose to include thanks to individuals or groups of people who have helped in the care of their child.

An example of a service sheet follows the Appendices.

Transporting the coffin

The coffin may be carried in a hearse provided by the funeral director.

An ordinary estate car may be more appropriate for a small coffin.

The car does not have to be black. White or another colour may be more suitable.

The family may choose to use their own car or to borrow one from a friend.

In some places it is traditional to use a horse-drawn hearse.

The funeral director may walk in front of the hearse for part of the journey.

In a village the coffin may sometimes be carried without needing to use a hearse or car.

The cortège may pause as a mark of respect at particular places, for example outside the child's home if the journey has begun somewhere else.

It may be important for the family to decide with the funeral director whether the coffin will be carried or wheeled into the place where the funeral service will take place and who will do this.

Carrying the coffin into church the night before the funeral

In some Christian traditions this has been common practice for centuries. To some parents it may be comforting – as if it symbolises that their child is a step closer on the journey to heaven.

It may provide an opportunity for the father, both parents or other members of the immediate family to carry the coffin into church themselves. For some the ordeal of doing this in front of the whole congregation at the funeral service may be too great.

Simple prayers may be offered as the child is brought into the church. The coffin, depending on the size, may be placed on a table or on a bier, in a suitable place in the church. Flowers may be placed on the coffin or around it. A candle, perhaps the Easter candle, may be left burning close to the coffin. Light in the darkness can be comforting on a practical as well as a symbolic level.

This occasion may be attended only by the parents and the minister of religion or by anyone the parents may invite. If the building is normally locked overnight, it may be kind to offer to lend the key to the family.

Recording the service

A tape recording of the funeral service may be a source of great consolation in the months and years which follow. There may well be times when members of the family find it too painful to listen to the tape. Some may never want to do so. But if a recording has been made then they have the choice. This is something which a friend or relative may be asked to do, or the funeral director will arrange for the recording to be made.

Who comes to the funeral?

Parents may choose to make an open invitation to anyone who would like to attend the funeral.

They may choose to keep some part of it private, for example:

– bringing the coffin into church the night before;
– committal of the body at the crematorium;
– burial at the grave side.

They may invite others to join them for the remainder of the service.

Another possibility is to have a private funeral service followed, at a later date, by a memorial service or service of thanksgiving.

Many adults worry about whether it is right to bring children – brothers, sisters, cousins, friends – to the funeral service. This is a very personal decision but, where at all possible, it does seem sensible to ask the child himself or herself. To be included usually feels better than to be excluded, even in the presence of raw grief, but some will have their own reasons for not wanting to be there.

If, for whatever reason, children are not present at the funeral, it may be important for them to be doing something significant at the time of the funeral so that they do not feel left out, guilty or empty. This could be visiting a special place, listening to favourite music, drawing or painting with someone with whom they feel comfortable.

It may be difficult for the family to remember who was present at the funeral, so those who attend may be asked to sign on a sheet of paper or a book either when they arrive before the service begins or before they leave. The funeral director or a friend will be responsible for this if asked.

Reception after the funeral

Some families will want to invite those who attend the funeral to return to the family home or the house of a relative or friend for refreshments afterwards. Some may prefer to meet in a hotel, pub or restaurant.

Preparing the food and drink may be one way in which relatives and friends can help. Alternatively a catering firm may be employed.

People often find it hard to know what to say on such an

occasion. They should not be afraid of talking about the child who has died.

Parents may prefer to be alone or with the immediate family only after the service and relatives and friends will understand and respect this.

What Friends Can Do

Practical ways in which friends may help

These are many and varied. A basic list is given, to which many suggested ways of helping may be added.

- calling on the family
- cooking for them
- offering to wash clothes or bed linen
- doing some housework
- shopping
- driving
- being with other children in the family
- informing named relatives or friends of the death and the funeral arrangements
- preparing refreshments to be offered to relatives and friends after the funeral
- making a tape recording of the funeral service
- listening and not 'doing' anything.

As the weeks go by the needs of the bereaved family will often become greater rather than less. The most urgent need will be for someone who will listen without giving advice or referring to any experience they themselves may have had, except in so far as it may serve to convince the grieving person that he or she is normal in grieving this way. Anger is an integral part of grief and the friend must be prepared to be a receptacle for that anger without necessarily colluding with it. One subject bereaved people often want to talk about is the person who has died, yet so often it is the last subject other people want to broach. It is helpful to give the bereaved person the opportunity of talking about the child who has died.

Grief is an exhausting process, exhausting physically, mentally, emotionally and spiritually. Remembering this, good friends will find many ways of helping through the months and years of acute bereavement. Grief following the death of a child may go on getting worse for two years or more. In a society which expects you to be 'back to normal' in six weeks, the reality can quickly leave the child's family believing they are either sick or abnormal – 'Am I going mad?'

Loss of identity or role is very painful – realising that you are no longer a parent, or that you have become an 'only child'.

Friends who will stay alongside, recognising the right of the grieving person to grieve in his or her own way, knowing that no two people, however loving or close they may be, grieve in the same way, are invaluable. It is usually a help rather than a hindrance when a friend shows his or her own true feelings. Bereaved parents or brothers or sisters know that other people are embarrassed or frightened of saying the wrong thing. It is often enough to say, 'I am so very sorry', or, 'How are you?' and then wait long enough to hear the honest answer.

Many families welcome friends' recognition of the anniversaries of the child's birth and death and difficult times such as Christmas, Mother's Day or Father's Day. Friends need not fear reminding the family; they will not have forgotten and may well feel comforted and supported that others have not forgotten either.

Unhelpful things to say or do

Euphemisms – 'falling asleep', 'passed away', 'lost' – are normally unhelpful. 'He has died' is true and straightforward and not offensive.

In all the pain and confusion it is easy to resort to clichés when talking to newly bereaved families. For example.

'God took her because she was so special.'
'Jesus has called him to be a little sun-beam . . .'

'God needed another baby angel.'

'It's a mercy – with his handicap he could never have lived a full life.'

'Time will heal.'

'At least you have got the other children.'

'You're young enough to have more.'

'She's gone to sleep with Jesus.'

'He's looking down on us from heaven.'

These examples could be multiplied. There may be elements of truth in some of the remarks, but those who grieve the death of their children are unlikely to find any help and comfort in them, unless they themselves introduce the idea.

The anguish of separation is overwhelming. It feels as if half of them has been amputated. Can they survive?

Belief in God may bring comfort and consolation but it may also bring confusion and anger. There are far more questions than answers. It is unhelpful to try to fill the yawning abyss of unknowing with easy answers.

The real friend will stay alongside, often silent, through all the unknowing, the anger and accusations, the guilt, the if-onlys. Guilt is powerful and overwhelming – about surviving beyond the death of your child; about not preventing that death or even in some way causing it; guilt the first time you laugh or live through an hour without thinking about your child. Raw grief is neither reasonable nor rational all the time. It operates at a level much deeper than the intellect.

To stay alongside a grieving person means listening to the same part of the story again and again without trying to correct it.

Do not tell people how they should be grieving.

Each person has his or her own way of grieving. Even those who are very close to one another will grieve differently.

In the state of exhaustion brought about by grief it may or may not be helpful to suggest a game of tennis or joining a drama group. Do not make people feel that they *ought* to do something because it would 'do you good'.

Do not avoid coming face to face with a bereaved person out

of fear or embarrassment. If you cannot find the right words then a hug, a touch or even a smile will help.

Deciding what to do with clothes, toys and other things which have belonged to the child, and re-arranging the bedroom should only be done when the parents are ready. There is no hurry. It may be years rather than days or months before they are ready. This is normal.

Part Two

Prayers

Almighty God, Father of all mercies and giver of all comfort: Deal graciously, we pray thee, with those who mourn, that casting every care on thee, they may know the consolation of thy love; through Jesus Christ our Lord.

From the Prayer Book as Proposed in 1928

Almighty God, giver of every good and perfect gift, we thank you for the happiness and love this child has brought and for the assurance we have that she/he is in your care. Strengthen us to commit ourselves to your gracious providence, so that we may live our lives here in the peace and joy of faith, until at the last we are united with all the children of God in the brightness of your glory, through Jesus Christ our Lord.

Pauline Webb

Bring us O Lord God at our last awakening into the house and gate of Heaven, to enter into that house where there shall be no darkness nor dazzling, but one equal light; no noise nor silence, but one equal music; no fears or hopes, but one equal possession; no ends nor beginnings, but one equal eternity in the habitations of Thy Glory and Dominion, world without end.

Based on John Donne

Father in heaven, healer of the broken-hearted, look in pity and compassion upon your servants whose joy has been turned into mourning. Comfort them and grant that they may be drawn closer to each other by their common sorrow. Dwell with them and be their refuge until the day break and the shadows flee away; through Jesus Christ our Lord. Amen.

From the Funeral Service for a Child Dying Near the Time of Birth

Father, the death of N brings an emptiness into our lives.
We are separated from her/him
and feel broken and disturbed.
Give us confidence that s/he is safe
and her/his life complete with you.
Help us by your constant presence to know
that Jesus bridges the gap
between death and life.
This we ask through Jesus Christ our Lord.
Amen.

From A New Zealand Prayer Book, He Karakia Mihinare o Aotearoa

Father,
You know our hearts and share our sorrows.
We are hurt from our parting
from N whom we loved:
When we are angry at the loss we have sustained,
when we long for words of comfort,
yet find them hard to bear,
turn our grief into truer living,
our affliction into firmer hope
and our sorrow to deeper joy.

From the General Synod of the Scottish Episcopal Church's Revised Funeral Rites

Forgiving God,
in the face of death we discover
how many things are still undone,

how much might have been done otherwise.
Redeem our failure.
Bind up the wounds of past mistakes.
Transform our guilt to active love,
and by your forgiveness make us whole.

From the General Synod of the Scottish Episcopal Church's Revised Funeral Rites

Gentle Lord,
your servant has come
by a hard and painful road
into the valley of death.
Lead him/her now into the place
where there is no more pain.

From the General Synod of the Scottish Episcopal Church's Revised Funeral Rites.

God be in my head, and in my understanding;
 God be in mine eyes, and in my looking;
God be in my mouth, and in my speaking;
 God be in my heart, and in my thinking;
God be at mine end, and at my departing.

Sarum Prayer

God of all compassion,
you make nothing in vain
and love all you have created.
Comfort (these) your servants (*NN*)
whose hearts are weighed down by grief and sorrow.
Lift them up,
and grant that they may so love and serve you in this life,
that together with *N*,
your child and theirs,
they may obtain the fullness of your promises
in the age to come;

through Jesus Christ our Lord.
Amen.

From A New Zealand Prayer Book, He Karakia Mihinare o Aotearoa

After a short life
God of all mystery, whose ways are beyond understanding,
lead us, who grieve at this untimely death,
to a new and deeper faith in your love
which brought your Son Jesus,
the young prince of glory,
into resurrection life.

From the General Synod of the Scottish Episcopal Church's Revised Funeral Rites

God of the living and the dead,
when you raised Jesus from the tomb
you gave new hope to his desolate disciples.
Cleanse, restore and heal us
in our time of sorrow.
May we go forward in his strength upon our pilgrimage,
sharing the fellowship of the redeemed, both living and
   departed.

From the General Synod of the Scottish Episcopal Church's Revised Funeral Rites

For a still-born child
God our Creator,
from whom all life comes,
comfort this family,
grieving for the loss of their hoped-for child.
Help them to find assurance
that with you nothing is wasted or incomplete,
and uphold them with your love,
through Jesus Christ our Saviour,
Amen.

From A New Zealand Prayer Book, He Karakia Mihinare o Aotearoa

God our Creator,
you called into being this fragile life, which to us had seemed
    so full of promise:
Give to N whom we commit to your care,
fullness of life in your presence,
and to us, who grieve over hopes unfulfilled,
courage to bear our loss;
through Jesus Christ our Lord. Amen.

From the General Synod of the Scottish Episcopal Church's Revised Funeral Rites

God, we are told that you are compassionate,
today this is hard to believe.
God, we are told that you love us,
today we do not feel loved.
God, we are told that we should offer you our praise and
    thanksgivings,
today all we have to offer is anger and confusion.
God, despite these feelings we turn to you,
today there is no one else to turn to.
God, hold us until we can believe again.
God, love us until we can feel your love again.
God, accept our anger and confusion until we can offer you
    praise and thanksgivings again.
God, our lives and our feelings rise and fall but you remain
    constant.
Help us to rest in your eternal changelessness. Amen.

Michael D. Smith

Go forth upon thy journey, Christian soul!
Go from this world! Go, in the Name of God
The Omnipotent Father, who created thee!
Go, in the Name of Jesus Christ, our Lord,
Son of the Living God, who bled for thee!
Go, in the Name of the Holy Spirit, who
Hath been poured out on thee! Go, in the name

Of Angels and Archangels; in the name
Of Thrones and Dominations; in the name
Of Princedoms and of Powers; and in the name
Of Cherubim and Seraphim, go forth!
Go, in the name of Patriarchs and Prophets;
And of Apostles and Evangelists,
Of Martyrs and Confessors; in the name
Of holy Monks and Hermits; in the name
Of holy Virgins; and all Saints of God,
Both men and women, go! Go on thy course;
And may thy place to-day be found in peace,
And may thy dwelling be the Holy Mount
Of Sion: – through the Same, through Christ, our Lord.

John Henry Newman, based on the traditional Western Commendation of a Soul.

Gracious Father,
in darkness and in light,
in trouble and in joy,
help us to trust your love,
to serve your purpose,
and to praise your name;
through Jesus Christ our Lord. Amen.

From the Funeral Service for a Child Dying Near the Time of Birth

Grant, O Lord, that we may walk in your presence, with your
love in our hearts, your trust in our minds, your strength in
our wills: that when we finally stand before you, it may be with
the assurance of your welcome and the joy of our homecoming.
And the blessing of God Almighty, the Father, the Son and the
Holy Spirit rest upon you and be with you, now and always.

Prayer for those with broken hearts

Grieving, Jesus wept at the tomb of a beloved friend.

Alone, Jesus agonised in confusion and isolation in the Garden
of Gethsemane.

Broken hearted, Jesus cried out in pain and anguish as he
died.

Almighty God, today we bring to you our grief and tears,
our loneliness and confusion,

our anguish and pain,

our broken hearts.

We pray that as you held Jesus in your love throughout his
dark days

and brought him to new life on the first Easter day,

so you will hold us in these dark hours of ours

and, in time, bring us to new life.

We offer this prayer in the name of Jesus. Amen.

Michael D. Smith

In the rising of the sun
and in its going down
We remember them/her/him

In the blowing of the wind
and in the chill of winter
We remember them/her/him

In the opening of buds
and in the warmth of summer
We remember them/her/him

In the rustling of leaves
and in the beauty of autumn
We remember them/her/him

In the beginning of the year
and when it ends
We remember them/her/him.

Gates of Prayer, Reform Judaism Prayer Book

Lord Jesus Christ, you care for little children in this present life and have prepared for them in the life to come a home where they behold your Father's face. Make us assuredly to know that you have received *N* in peace. For you have said, Let the children come to me, for to such belongs the kingdom of heaven. To you, with the Father and the Holy Spirit, be all glory, honour and worship, now and ever, world without end.

Lord Jesus,
we ask you to be close to the children of this family,
whose lives have been changed by sorrow.
Give them courage to face their loss,
and comfort them with your unchanging love.
Amen.

From A New Zealand Prayer Book, He Karakia Mihinare o Aotearoa

Lord Jesus Christ,
you took children into your arms
and blessed them.
Keep this child in your loving care
and bring us all to the heavenly kingdom,
where you live and reign
with the Father and the Holy Spirit now and forever.
Amen.

From A New Zealand Prayer Book, He Karakia Minihare o Aotearoa

Lord, make me a channel of Thy peace; where there is hatred may I bring love; where there is injury, pardon; where there is doubt, faith; where there is despair, hope; where there is darkness, light; and where there is sadness, joy. O Divine Lover, grant that we may not so much seek to be consoled as to console; to be understood as to understand; to be loved as to love; for it is in giving that we receive, it is in pardoning that we are pardoned, and it is in dying that we are born to eternal life.

St Francis of Assisi (attributed)

Lord of all, we thank you
for your work in creation,
for nourishing life in the womb,
for your love even in death.
Thank you for the life of this child *N*,
whom you gave to us and have taken to yourself.
Thank you for the arms of your love
embracing both us and *N* in your family.
Thank you for your presence in our sorrow
and your strength as our family grows older.
Take our sadness, and fill us with your Spirit
to serve you on earth
and join your saints in glory,
through Jesus Christ our Lord. Amen.

From the Funeral Service for a Child Dying Near the Time of Birth

Lord we pray for the bereaved, asking that their heartbreak may be healed by the balm of God's comfort, and that beyond the dreadful silence of death they may hear the songs of the angels bringing the hope of heaven. Through Jesus Christ our Lord.

Pauline Webb

Lord, we turn to You in our grief and our bewilderment, for a mystery surrounds the birth and death of man. Your will summons us into this world and then calls us to depart, but Your plan is so vast and Your purposes so deep that our understanding fails, and our reason cannot follow. Yet You have taught us that time and space are not the measure of all things. Beyond them is the life of eternity. We do not die into the grave but into the love of God.

It has been Your will to receive the soul of *N*, to bring her/him to life everlasting, and she/he is beyond the tragedies of this world. We find our comfort in Your teaching. Beyond the grave we shall meet together in the life that has no end.

Jewish Funeral Service Prayer Book

Lord, without our consent we are born, without our consent we live, without our consent we die, without our consent our bodies return to the grave and our spirit goes forward to life everlasting. We cannot always understand Your plans and we do not see Your ways, for our minds are overwhelmed and our eyes are too weak. Yet to comfort us and give us hope You lift the veil of eternity, and we are permitted to know that the world is a corridor, and we are on a journey, that the end is perfection, and the reward is peace.

For a short time You gave into our care a child whom we loved. Our hearts would be broken if we did not know that You are love itself, which makes good all that is lost. The tears would never leave our eyes if we did not know that at the end You bring all together, with mercy and tenderness, in the gathering of life. Therefore with sadness and with hope we commend the soul of *N* into your care. You are with her/him, we cannot fear.

Jewish Funeral Service Prayer Book

O Father of all, we pray to thee for those whom we love, but see no longer. Grant them thy peace; let light perpetual shine upon them; and in thy loving wisdom and almighty power, work in them the good purpose of thy perfect will; through Jesus Christ our Lord.

From the Prayer Book as Proposed in 1928

O God the King of glory, who hast exalted thine only Son Jesus Christ with great triumph unto thy kingdom in heaven: We beseech thee, leave us not comfortless; but send to us thine Holy Ghost to comfort us, and exalt us unto the same place whither our Saviour Christ is gone before, who liveth and reigneth with thee and the Holy Ghost, one God, world without end.

Book of Common Prayer

O Lord, God of the spirits of all flesh, You are with us at all times: in joy and in sorrow, in light and in darkness, in life and in death. Open our hearts, that we may feel Your presence even at this hour of bereavement. Let the knowledge of Your nearness soothe our spirits and heal our wounds. Teach us to trust You. We do not always understand your ways, but even as we grieve, make us grateful for the blessings we have received, and give us the faith to declare: The Lord gave, and the Lord has taken away; praised be the name of the Lord.

Jewish Funeral Service Prayer Book

O Lord, support us all the day long of this troublous life, until the shades lengthen, and the evening comes, and the busy world is hushed, the fever of life is over, and our work is done. Then, Lord, in Thy mercy, grant us safe lodging, a holy rest, and peace at the last; through our Lord Jesus Christ.

John Henry Newman

Please listen, God,
while we talk to you about *N* who has died.
Take care of *her/him*, and please take care of us too.
Thank you for the times we had together.
Thank you for Jesus, who shows us your love.
He is close to *N*, and he is close to us.
Thank you, God.
Amen.

From A New Zealand Prayer Book, He Karakia Mihinare o Aotearoa

Support us, Lord, when we are silent through grief! Comfort us when we are bent down with sorrow! Help us as we bear the weight of our loss! Lord, our Rock and our Redeemer, give us strength!

Jewish Funeral Service Prayer Book

We seem to give them back to Thee, O God, who gavest them to us. Yet, as Thou didst not lose them in giving, so do we not lose them by their return. Not as the world giveth, givest Thou, O Lover of souls. What Thou givest, Thou takest not away, for what is Thine is ours also if we are Thine. And life is eternal and love is immortal, and death is only an horizon, and an horizon is nothing save the limit of our sight. Lift us up, strong Son of God, that we may see further; cleanse our eyes that we may see more clearly; draw us closer to Thyself that we may know ourselves to be nearer to our loved ones who are with Thee. And while Thou dost prepare a place for us, prepare us also for that happy place, that where Thou art we may be also for evermore.

William Penn

When we are weary and in need of strength,
When we are lost and sick at heart,
We remember her/him.

When we have a joy we crave to share
When we have decisions that are difficult to make
When we have achievements that are based on hers/his
We remember her/him.

At the blowing of the wind and in the chill of winter
At the opening of the buds and in the rebirth of spring,
We remember her/him.

At the blueness of the skies and in the warmth of summer

At the rustling of the leaves and in the beauty of autumn,
We remember her/him.

At the rising of the sun and at its setting,
We remember her/him.

As long as we live, s/he too will live
For s/he is now a part of us,
As we remember her/him.

Adapted from the Yizkor Service, *Jewish Funeral Service* Prayer Book

A prayer for a loved one departed

You shared life with us: God give eternal life to you.
You gave your love to us: God give his deep love to you.
You gave your time to us: God give his eternity to you.
You gave your light to us: God give everlasting light to you.
Go upon your journey dear soul to love, light and life eternal.

David Adam

Blessings

Blessing of the body

The assembly is invited to bow their heads as the minister prays the final blessing:

Minister: We give you praise and we thank you, Father, for you formed our bodies from the dust of your beautiful creation, breathed into us your spirit, and gave us delight that we can see, smell and hear, that we can taste and touch. We praise you, Lord, for N, whose body was a temple of your Spirit, and we bless his/her body as we await the resurrection of the dead and the life of the world to come.

All: Amen.

Robert Eimer OMI and Sarah O'Malley OSB

Deep peace of the running wave to you
Deep peace of the flowing air to you
Deep peace of the quiet earth to you
Deep peace of the shining stars to you
Deep peace of the Son of Peace to you.

Traditional Gaelic Rune

May the road rise to meet you,
May the wind be always at your back,
May the sun shine warm upon your face,
May the rains fall softly upon your fields.
Until we meet again,
May God hold you in the hollow of his hand.

Gaelic prayer

The Lord bless you and keep you: the Lord make his face to shine
upon you, and be gracious unto you: the Lord lift up the light of
his countenance upon you, and give you peace.

Numbers 6:24–26 (Revised Standard Version of the Bible, Catholic Edition)

Act of farewell
Child of my flesh
bone of my bone
wherever you go, I will go,
wherever you live, I will live.
As you go into the mystery of life before us
may you be at peace.
That in God's good time
we may be together in peace.

SANDS (Stillbirth and Neonatal Death Society)

Scriptural Readings

These are set out in the order in which
they appear in the Bible

Psalm 23
The Lord is my shepherd,
I shall not want;
he makes me lie down in green pastures.
He leads me beside still waters;
he restores my soul.
He leads me in paths of righteousness
for his name's sake.

Even though I walk through the valley
of the shadow of death,
I fear no evil;
for thou art with me;
thy rod and thy staff,
they comfort me.

Thou preparest a table before me
in the presence of my enemies;
thou anointest my head with oil,
my cup overflows.

Surely goodness and mercy shall follow me
all the days of my life;
and I shall dwell in the house of the Lord for ever.

Revised Standard Version of the Bible, Catholic Edition

Psalm 84, verses 1–4
How lovely is thy dwelling place,
O Lord of hosts!
My soul longs, yea, faints
for the courts of the Lord;
my heart and flesh sing for joy
to the living God.

Even the sparrow finds a home,
and the swallow a nest for herself,
where she may lay her young,
at thy altars, O Lord of hosts,
my King and my God.
Blessed are those who dwell in thy house,
ever singing thy praise!

Revised Standard Version of the Bible, Catholic Edition

Psalm 121
I lift up my eyes to the hills.
From whence does my help come?
My help comes from the Lord,
who made heaven and earth.

He will not let your foot be moved,
he who keeps you will not slumber.
Behold, he who keeps Israel
will neither slumber nor sleep.
The Lord is your keeper;
the Lord is your shade
on your right hand.
The sun shall not smite you by day,
nor the moon by night.

The Lord will keep you from all evil;
he will keep your life.
The Lord will keep

your going out and your coming in
from this time forth and for evermore.

Revised Standard Version of the Bible, Catholic Edition

Song of Songs Chapter 2, verses 10–13

My beloved answered, he said to me:
Rise up, my darling;
my fairest, come away.
For now the winter is past,
the rains are over and gone;
the flowers appear in the country-side;
the time is coming when the birds will sing,
and the turtle-dove's cooing will be heard in our land;
when the green figs will ripen on the fig-trees
and the vines give forth their fragrance.
Rise up, my darling;
my fairest, come away.

New English Bible

Isaiah Chapter 49, verses 15–16

Can a woman forget her baby at the breast,
feel no pity for the child she has borne?
Even if these were to forget,
I shall not forget you.
Look, I have engraved you on the palms of my hands.

New Jerusalem Bible

The Gospel according to St Matthew, Chapter 18, verses 1–5 and 10

At that time the disciples came to Jesus and asked, 'Who is the greatest in the kingdom of Heaven?' He called a child, set him in front of them, and said, 'I tell you this: unless you turn round and become like children, you will never enter the kingdom of

Heaven. Let a man humble himself till he is like this child, and he will be greatest in the kingdom of Heaven . . .

'Never despise one of these little ones; I tell you, they have their guardian angels in Heaven, who look continually on the face of my heavenly Father.'

New English Bible

The Gospel according to St Matthew, chapter 19, verses 13–15

Then people brought little children to him, for him to lay his hands on them and pray. The disciples scolded them, but Jesus said, 'Let the children alone, and do not stop them from coming to me; for it is to such as these that the kingdom of Heaven belongs.' Then he laid his hands on them and went on his way.

New Jerusalem Bible

The Gospel according to St Mark, chapter 10, verses 14–17

He said to them, 'Let the children come to me; do not try to stop them; for the kingdom of God belongs to such as these. I tell you, whoever does not accept the kingdom of God like a child, will never enter it.' And he put his arms round them, laid his hands upon them, and blessed them.

New English Bible

The Gospel according to St Mark, Chapter 16, verses 1–7

When the Sabbath was over, Mary of Magdala, Mary the mother of James, and Salome, bought spices with which to go and anoint him. And very early in the morning on the first day of the week they went to the tomb when the sun had risen.

They had been saying to one another, 'Who will roll away the stone for us from the entrance to the tomb?' But when they looked they saw that the stone – which was very big – had already been rolled back. On entering the tomb they saw a young man in a white robe seated on the right-hand side, and they were struck with amazement. But he said to them, 'There is no need to be so amazed. You are looking for Jesus of Nazareth, who was crucified: he is risen, he is not here. See, here is the place where they laid him. But you must go and tell his disciples and Peter, "He is going ahead of you to Galilee; that is where you will see him, just as he told you." '

New Jerusalem Bible

The Gospel according to St John, Chapter 3, verses 16 and 17

'God loved the world so much that he gave his only Son, that everyone who has faith in him may not die but have eternal life. It was not to judge the world that God sent his Son into the world, but that through him the world might be saved.'

New English Bible

From the Gospel according to St John, Chapter 14, verses 1–6

'Let not your hearts be troubled; believe in God, believe also in me. In my Father's house are many rooms; if it were not so, would I have told you that I go to prepare a place for you? And when I go and prepare a place for you, I will come again and will take you to myself, that where I am you may be also. And you know the way where I am going.' Thomas said to him, 'Lord, we do not know where you are going; how can we know the way?' Jesus said to him, 'I am the way, and the truth, and the life; no one comes to the Father, but by me.'

Revised Standard Version of the Bible, Catholic Edition

The Letter to the Romans, Chapter 8, verses 38 and 39

For I am sure that neither death, nor life, nor angels, nor principalities, nor things present, nor things to come, nor powers, nor height, nor depth, nor anything else in all creation, will be able to separate us from the love of God in Christ Jesus our Lord.

Revised Standard Version of the Bible, Catholic Edition

The Letter to the Romans, Chapter 14, verses 7 and 8

For no one of us lives, and equally no one of us dies, for himself alone. If we live, we live for the Lord; and if we die, we die for the Lord. Whether therefore we live or die, we belong to the Lord.

New English Bible

First Letter to the Corinthians, Chapter 13, verses 1–13

If I speak in the tongues of men and of angels, but have not love, I am a noisy gong or a clanging cymbal. And if I have prophetic powers, and understand all mysteries and all knowledge, and if I have all faith, so as to remove mountains, but have not love, I am nothing. If I give away all I have, and if I deliver my body to be burned, but have not love, I gain nothing.

Love is patient and kind; love is not jealous or boastful; it is not arrogant or rude. Love does not insist on its own way; it is not irritable or resentful; it does not rejoice at wrong, but rejoices in the right. Love bears all things, believes all things, hopes all things, endures all things.

Love never ends; as for prophecies, they will pass away; as for tongues, they will cease; as for knowledge, it will pass away. For our knowledge is imperfect and our prophecy is imperfect; but when the perfect comes, the imperfect will pass away. When I was a child, I spoke like a child, I thought like a child, I reasoned like a child; when I became a man, I gave up childish ways. For now we see in a mirror dimly, but then face to face. Now I know in part; then I shall understand fully, even as I have been fully understood. So faith, hope, love abide, these three: but the greatest of these is love.

Revised Standard Version of the Bible, Catholic Edition

First Letter to the Corinthians, Chapter 15, verses 35–57

Someone may ask: How are dead people raised, and what sort of body do they have when they come? How foolish! What you sow must die before it is given new life; and what you sow is not the body that is to be, but only a bare grain, of wheat I dare say, or some other kind; it is God who gives it the sort of body that he has chosen for it, and for each kind of seed its own kind of body.

Not all flesh is the same flesh: there is human flesh; animals have another kind of flesh, birds another and fish yet another. Then there are heavenly bodies and earthly bodies; the heavenly have a splendour of their own, and the earthly a different splendour. The sun has its own splendour, the moon another splendour, and the stars yet another splendour; and the stars differ among themselves in splendour. It is the same too with the resurrection of the dead: what is sown is perishable, but what is raised is imperishable; what is sown is contemptible but what is raised is glorious; what is sown is weak, but what is raised is powerful; what is sown is a natural body, and what is raised is a spiritual body.

If there is a natural body, there is a spiritual body too. So the first man, Adam, as scripture says, became a living soul; and the last Adam has become a life-giving spirit. But first came the natural body, not the spiritual one; that came only afterwards. The first man, being made of earth, is earthly by nature; the second man is from heaven. The earthly man is the pattern for all earthly people, the heavenly man for heavenly ones. And as we have borne the likeness of the earthly man, so we shall bear the likeness of the heavenly one.

What I am saying, brothers, is that mere human nature cannot inherit the kingdom of God: what is perishable cannot inherit what is imperishable. Now I am going to tell you a mystery: we are not all going to fall asleep, but we are all going to be changed, instantly, in the twinkling of an eye, when the last trumpet sounds. The trumpet is going to sound, and then the dead will be raised imperishable, and we shall be changed, because this perishable nature of ours must put on imperishability, this mortal nature must put on immortality.

And after this perishable nature has put on imperishability and this mortal nature has put on immortality, then will the words of scripture come true: Death is swallowed up in victory. Death, where is your victory? Death, where is your sting? The sting of death is sin, and the power of sin comes from the Law. Thank God, then, for giving us the victory through Jesus Christ our Lord.

New Jerusalem Bible

The Letter to the Ephesians, Chapter 3, verses 14–19

With this in mind, then, I kneel in prayer to the Father, from whom every family in heaven and on earth takes its name, that out of the treasures of his glory he may grant you strength and power through his Spirit in your inner being, that through faith, Christ may dwell in your hearts in love. With deep roots and firm foundations, may you be strong to grasp, with all God's people, what is the breadth and length and height and depth of the love of Christ, and to know it, though it is beyond knowledge. So may you attain to fullness of being, the fullness of God himself.

New English Bible

First Letter to the Thessalonians, Chapter 4, verses 13–18

We want you to be quite certain, brothers, about those who have fallen asleep to make sure that you do not grieve for them, as others do who have no hope. We believe that Jesus died and rose again, and that in the same way God will bring with him those who have fallen asleep in Jesus. We can tell you this from the Lord's own teaching, that we who are still alive for the Lord's coming will not have any advantage over those who have fallen asleep. At the signal given by the voice of the Archangel and the trumpet of God, the Lord himself will come down from heaven; those who have died in Christ will be the first to rise, and only after that shall we who remain alive be taken up in the clouds, together with them, to meet the Lord in the air. This is the way we shall be with the Lord for ever. With such thoughts as these, then, you should encourage one another.

New Jerusalem Bible

The Revelation of St John, Chapter 21, verses 1–7

Then I saw a new heaven and a new earth; for the first heaven and the first earth had passed away, and the sea was no more. And I saw the holy city, new Jerusalem, coming down out of heaven from God, prepared as a bride adorned for her husband; and I heard a great voice from the throne saying, 'Behold, the dwelling of God is with men. He will dwell with them, and they shall be his people, and God himself will be with them; he will wipe away every tear from their eyes, and death shall be no more, neither shall there be mourning nor crying nor pain any more, for the former things have passed away.'

And he who sat upon the throne said, 'Behold, I make all things new.' Also he said, 'Write this, for these words are trustworthy and true.' And he said to me, 'It is done! I am the Alpha and the Omega, the beginning and the end. To the thirsty I will give water without price from the fountain of the water of life. He who conquers shall have this heritage, and I will be his God, and he will be my son.'

Revised Standard Version of the Bible, Catholic Edition

The Revelation of St John Chapter 22, verses 1–5

Then he showed me the river of the water of life, bright as crystal, flowing from the throne of God and of the Lamb through the middle of the street of the city; also, on either side of the river, the tree of life with its twelve kinds of fruit, yielding its fruit each month; and the leaves of the tree were for the healing of the nations. There shall no more be anything accursed, but the throne of God and of the Lamb shall be in it, and his servants shall worship him; they shall see his face, and his name shall be on their foreheads. And night shall be no more; they need no light of lamp or sun, for the Lord God will be their light, and they shall reign for ever and ever.

Revised Standard Version of the Bible, Catholic Edition

Non-Scriptural Readings

They came in the evening then, and found Jonathan gliding peaceful and alone through his beloved sky. The two gulls that appeared at his wings were pure as starlight, and the glow from them was gentle and friendly in the high night air. But most lovely of all was the skill with which they flew, their wingtips moving a precise and constant inch from his own.

Without a word, Jonathan put them to his test, a test that no gull had ever passed. He twisted his wings, slowed to a single mile per hour above stall. The two radiant birds slowed with him, smoothly, locked in position. They knew about slow flying.

He folded his wings, rolled, and dropped in a dive to a hundred and ninety miles per hour. They dropped with him, streaking down in flawless formation.

At last he turned that speed straight up into a long vertical slow roll. They rolled with him, smiling.

He recovered to level flight and was quiet for a time before he spoke. 'Very well', he said, 'who are you?'

'We're from your flock, Jonathan. We are your brothers.' The words were strong and calm. 'We've come to take you higher to take you home.'

'Home, I have none. Flock, I have none. I am Outcast. And we fly now at the peak of the Great Mountain Wind. Beyond a few hundred feet, I can lift this (old) body no higher.'

'But you can, Jonathan. For you have learned. One school is finished, and the time has come for another to begin.'

As it had shined across him all his life, so understanding lighted the moment for Jonathan Seagull. They were right. He could fly higher, and it was time to go home.

He gave one last long look across the sky, across that magnificent silver land where he had learned so much.

'I'm ready,' he said at last.

And Jonathan Livingstone Seagull rose with the two star-bright gulls to disappear into a perfect dark sky.

So this is heaven, he thought, and he had to smile at himself. It was hardly respectful to analyse heaven in the very moment that one flies up to enter it.

As he came from Earth now, above the clouds and in close formation with the two brilliant gulls, he saw that his own body was growing as bright as theirs. True, the same young Jonathan Seagull was there that had always lived behind golden eyes, but the outer form had changed.

It felt like a seagull body, but already it flew far better than his old one had ever flown. Why, with half the effort, he thought, I'll get twice the speed, twice the performance of my best days on earth!'

His feathers glowed brilliant white now and his wings were smooth and perfect as sheets of polished silver. He began, delightedly, to learn about them, to press power into these new wings.

Richard Bach

To see a World in a Grain of Sand
And a Heaven in a Wild Flower,
Hold Infinity in the palm of your hand
And Eternity in an hour.

William Blake

Bonds
Nothing can fill that gap
When we are away from those we love
And it would be wrong to try and find anything
We must simply hold out and win through.
That sounds very hard at first.
But at the same time
It is a great consolation
Since leaving the gap unfilled
Preserves the bonds of love between us.
It is nonsense to say that God fills the gap.
He does not fill it but leaves it empty,
So that our communion with another may be kept alive
Even at the cost of pain.

Dietrich Bonhoeffer

Day that I have loved

Tenderly, day that I have loved, I close your eyes,
       And smooth your quiet brow, and fold your thin dead
           hands.
The grey veils of the half-light deepen; colour dies.
       I bear you, a light burden, to the shrouded sands,

Where lies your waiting boat, by wreaths of the sea's
           making
       Mist-garlanded, with all grey weeds of the water
           crowned.
There you'll be laid, past fear of sleep or hope of waking;
       And over the unmoving sea, without a sound,

Faint hands will row you outward, out beyond our sight,
       Us with stretched arms and empty eyes on the far-
           gleaming
And marble sand . . .
             Beyond the shifting cold twilight,
       Further than laughter goes, or tears, further than
           dreaming.

There'll be no port, no dawn-lit islands! But the drear
       Waste darkening, and, at length, flame ultimate on the
           deep.
Oh, the last fire – and you, unkissed, unfriended there!
       Oh, the lone way's red ending, and we not there to
           weep!

(We found you pale and quiet, and strangely crowned
         with flowers,
  Lovely and secret as a child. You came with us,
Came happily, hand in hand with the young dancing
         hours,
  High on the downs at dawn!) Void now and
        tenebrous,

The grey sands curve before me . . .
                    From the inland meadows,
   Fragrant of June and clover, floats the dark, and
            fills
The hollow sea's dead face with little creeping
            shadows,
   And the white silence brims the hollow of the hills.

Close in the next is folded every weary wing,
   Hushed all the joyful voices; and we, who held you
            dear,
Eastward we turn and homeward, alone,
            remembering . . .
            Day that I loved, day that I loved, the Night is here!

Rupert Brooke

When the last sunshine of expiring day
In summer's twilight weeps itself away,
Who has not felt the softness of the hour
Sink in the heart, as dew along the flower?
With a pure feeling which absorbs and awes
While nature makes that melancholy pause,
Her breathing moment on the bridge where Time
Of light and darkness forms an arch sublime,
Who hath not shared that calm, so still and deep,
The voiceless thought which would not speak but weep,
A holy concord, and a bright regret,
A glorious sympathy with suns that set?
'Tis not harsh sorrow, but a tenderer woe,
Nameless, but dear to gentle hearts below,
Felt without bitterness, but full and clear,
Estranged dejection, a transparent tear.
Unmixed with worldly grief or selfish strain,
Shed without shame, and secret without pain.

Even as the tenderness that hour instils,
When summer's day declines along the hills,
So feels the fulness of our heart and eyes,
When all of Youth which can perish dies
A soaring spirit is eclipsed – a power
Hath passed from day to darkness – at which hour
Pure light and likeness is bequeathed – new form
Gathering at once the rays of dawn.

George Gordon, Lord Byron (adapted)

We cannot judge a biography by its length, by the number of
pages in it: we must judge by the richness of the contents . . .
Sometimes the 'unfinisheds' are among the most beautiful sym-
phonies.

Victor Frankl

'Mister God made everything, didn't he?'

There was no point in saying that I didn't really know. I said
'Yes'.

'Even the dirt and the stars and the animals and the people and
the trees and everything, and the pollywogs?' The pollywogs were
those little creatures that we had seen under the microscope.

I said, 'Yes, he made everything.'

She nodded her agreement. 'Does Mister God love us truly?'

'Sure thing', I said. 'Mister God loves everything.'

'Oh', she said. 'Well then, why does he let things get hurt and
dead?' Her voice sounded as if she felt she had betrayed a sacred
trust, but the question had been thought and it had to be spoken.

'I don't know', I replied. 'There's a great many things about
Mister God that we don't know about.'

'Well then,' she continued, 'if we don't know many things
about Mister God, how do we know he loves us?'

I could see that this was going to be one of those times, but
thank goodness she didn't expect an answer to her question for

she hurried on: 'Them pollywogs, I could love them till I bust, but they wouldn't know, would they? I'm million times bigger than they are and Mister God is million times bigger than me, so how do I know what Mister God does?'

She was silent for a little while. Later I thought that at this moment she was taking her last look at babyhood. Then she went on:

'Fynn, Mister God doesn't love us.' She hesitated. 'He doesn't really, you know, only people can love. I love Bossy, but Bossy don't love me. I love the pollywogs, but they don't love me. I love you, Fynn, and you love me, don't you?'

I tightened my arm about her.

'You love me because you are people. I love Mister God truly, but he don't love me.'

It sounded to me like a death-knell. 'Damn and blast', I thought. 'Why does this have to happen to people? Now she's lost everything.' But I was wrong. She had got both feet planted firmly on the next stepping-stone.

'No,' she went on, 'no, he don't love me, not like you do, it's different, it's millions of times bigger.'

I must have made some movement or noise for she levered herself upright and sat on her haunches and giggled. Then she launched herself at me and undid my little pang of hurt, cut out the useless spark of jealousy with the delicate sureness of a surgeon.

'Fynn, you can love better than any people that ever was, and so can I, can't I? But Mister God is different. You see, Fynn, people can only love outside and can only kiss outside, but Mister God can love you right inside, and Mister God can kiss you right inside, so it's different. Mister God ain't like us; we are a little bit like Mister God, but not much yet.'

Fynn

And a woman who held a babe against her bosom said, 'Speak to us of Children.'
And he said: 'Your children are not your children,
They are the sons and daughters of Life's longing for itself.

They come through you but not from you,
And though they are with you,
Yet they belong not to you.

You may give them your love but not your thoughts,
For they have their own thoughts.
You may house their bodies but not their souls,
For their souls dwell in the house of tomorrow,
Which you cannot visit, not even in your dreams.
You may strive to be like them, but seek not to make them like
    you.
For life goes not backward nor tarries with yesterday.

You are the bows from which your children as living arrows are
    sent forth.
The Archer sees the mark upon the path of the infinite, and He
bends you with all His might, that His arrow may go swift and
    far.
Let your bending in the Archer's hand be for gladness;
For even as He loves the arrow that flies,
So He loves also the bow that is stable.

                                                    Kahlil Gibran

Then a woman said, 'Speak to us of Joy and Sorrow.'
And he answered:
'Your joy is your sorrow unmasked.
And the selfsame well from which your laughter rises was
    oftentimes filled with your tears.
And how else can it be?
The deeper that sorrow carves into your being, the more joy
    you can contain.
Is not the cup that holds your wine the very cup that was burned
    in the potter's oven?
And is not the lute that soothes your spirit the very wood that
    was hollowed by knives?

When you are joyous, look deep into your heart and you shall
    find it

is only that which has given you sorrow that is giving you joy.'

Kahlil Gibran

Life and death are one, even as the river and the sea are one.
In the depth of your hopes and desires lies your silent knowledge
   of the beyond;
And like seeds dreaming beneath the snow your heart dreams
   of spring.
Trust the dreams, for in them is hidden the gate to eternity . . .

For what is it to die but to stand naked in the wind and to melt
   into the sun?
And what is it to cease breathing but to free the breath from its
   restless tides, that it may rise and expand and seek God
   unencumbered?
Only when you drink from the river of silence shall you indeed
   sing.
And when you have reached the mountain top, then you shall
   begin to climb.
And when the earth shall claim your limbs, then shall you truly
   dance.

Kahlil Gibran

Farewell my friends
It was beautiful
As long as it lasted
The journey of my life.

I have no regrets
Whatsoever save
The pain I'll leave behind.

Those dear hearts
Who love and care
And the heavy with sleep

Ever moist eyes
The smile inspite of a
Lump in the throat
And the strings pulling
At the heart and soul.

The strong arms
That held me up
When my own strength
Let me down
Each morsel that I was
Fed with was full of love divine.

At every turning of my life
I came across
Good friends
Friends who stood by me
Even when the time raced me by.

Farewell
Farewell
My friends

I smile and
Bid you goodbye
No, shed no tears
For I need them not
All I need is your smile.

If you feel sad
Do think of me
For that's what I'll like
When you live in the hearts
Of those you love
Remember then . . .
You never die.

Gitanjali

I pray today

I pray today
in all earnestness
with all my heart and soul
for those whose hands
have reared me
and held me close
for those who have caressed
and eased my pain
and borne the suffering with me;
for those whose hearts
have wept in grief
and yet
sung happy songs to me;
for those who show
the patience rare
and help me
to keep my cool;
for those who dwell
in my bruised heart
and keep me wrapped
with the warmth of their love.
How can any harm
come to me,
when I am protected
with an armour of love.

Gitanjali

If I should go before the rest of you
Break not a flower nor inscribe a stone,
Nor when I'm gone speak in a Sunday voice
But be the usual selves that I have known,
Weep if you must,
Parting is hell,
But life goes on
So sing as well.

Joyce Grenfell

Memories – tender, loving, bittersweet
They can never be taken from you,
Nothing can detract from the joy
And the beauty you and your loved one shared.

Your love for the person and his or her love
for you cannot be altered by time or circumstance.
The memories are yours to keep.
Yesterday has ended, though you
Store it in the treasurehouse of the past.

Earl Grollman

I said to the man who stood at the Gate of the Year, 'Give me a
light that I may tread safely into the unknown.' And he replied,
'Go out into the darkness and put your hand into the hand of
God. That shall be to you better than light and safer than a known
way.'

Minnie Haskyns

Loving hands
I had a sorrow so deep
that human love could not penetrate
its deepest recesses.
I stumbled through the valley
of suffering in my mind,
down, down into the depths of the darkness.
And there in the tearless pain beyond pain
I saw two hands outstretched.
Two pierced hands –
that was all I could see –
two pierced hands held out to me.

I knew that my sorrow was shared
to the uttermost,
that I did not stand alone in the darkness,

that every part of my pain was understood.
Two loving hands –
that was all I could see –
two loving hands held out to me.

I felt no lessening of pain.
The stark reality of sorrow was still there,
to be faced and lived with.
But I was not alone.
In healing silence
two pierced hands had held mine
in the depths of that darkness.
Two sharing hands –
that was all I had seen –
two sharing hands held out to me.

Mary Hathaway

Love is this
That you lived amongst us these few years
And taught us love.

Love is this
That you died amongst us and helped us
To the source of life.

With all our love
We wish you bon voyage.

Love lives.

Lindy Hemmy

Death is nothing at all . . . I have only slipped away into the next
room. I am I, and you are you. Whatever we were to each other,
that we are still. Call me by my old familiar name. Speak to me
in the easy way which you always used. Put no differences into

your tone. Wear no forced air of solemnity or sorrow. Laugh as we always laughed at the little jokes we enjoyed together. Play, smile, think of me. Let my name be ever the household name that it always was. Let it be spoken without effort, without the ghost of a shadow on it. Life means all that it ever meant. It is the same as it always was. There is absolutely unbroken continuity. What is this death but a negligible accident? Why should I be out of mind because I am out of sight? I am waiting for you for an interval somewhere very near . . . just around the corner. All is well.

Henry Scott Holland

I am standing upon that foreshore. A ship at my side spreads her white sails to the morning breeze and starts for the blue ocean. She is an object of beauty and strength and I stand and watch her until at length she hangs like a speck of white cloud just where the sea and sky come down to mingle with each other. Then someone at my side says, 'There! She's gone!' 'Gone where?' 'Gone from my sight, that's all.' She is just as large in mast and spar and hull as ever she was when she left my side; just as able to bear her load of living freight to the place of her destination. Her diminished size is in me, not in her. And just at that moment when someone at my side says, 'There! She's gone!' there are other eyes watching her coming and other voices ready to take up the glad shout, 'Here she comes!' And that is dying.

Victor Hugo (a passage often attributed to Bishop Brent)

May He give us all the courage that we need to go the way He shepherds us. That, when He calls us, we may go unfrightened. If He bids us come to Him across the waters, that unfrightened we may go. And if He bids us climb the hill, may we not notice that it is a hill, mindful only of the happiness of His company . . . He made us for Himself, that we should travel with Him and see Him

at last in His unveiled beauty in the abiding city where He is light
and happiness and endless home.

Bede Jarrett OP

It is not growing like a tree
In bulk, doth make man better be;
Or standing long an oak, three hundred year,
To fall a log at last, dry, bald, and sere:
A lily of a day
Is fairer far in May,
Although it fall and die that night,
It was the plant and flower of light.
In small proportions we just beauty see,
And in short measures life may perfect be.

Ben Jonson

You bereaved are not alone. You belong to the largest company
in the world, the company of those who have known suffering.
When it seems that your sorrow is too great to be borne, think
of the great family of the heavy-hearted into which your grief has
given you entrance and, inevitably, you will feel about you their
arms, their sympathy, their understanding.

Helen Keller

Then Aslan turned to them and said:
    'You do not yet look so happy as I mean you to be.'
    Lucy said, 'We're so afraid of being sent away again, Aslan. And
you have sent us back into our world so often.'
    'No fear of that,' said Aslan. 'Have you not guessed?'
    Their hearts leaped and a wild hope rose within them.
    'There was a real railway accident,' said Aslan softly. 'Your father
and mother and all of you are, as you used to call it in the
Shadowland, dead. The term is over: the holidays have begun.
The dream is ended: this is the morning.'

And as He spoke He no longer looked to them like a lion; but the things that began to happen after that were so great and beautiful that I cannot write them. And for us this is the end of all the stories, and we can most truly say that they all lived happily ever after. But for them it was only the beginning of the real story. All their life in the world and all their adventures in Narnia had only been the cover and the title page: now at last they were beginning Chapter One of the Great Story which no one on earth has read; which goes on for ever and ever; in which every chapter is better than the one before.

C. S. Lewis

Death is not an end, but a beginning. It is but an incident in the 'life of the ages', which is God's gift to us *now.* It is the escape of the spirit from its old limitations and its freeing for a larger and more glorious career. We stand around the grave, and as we take our last, lingering look, too often our thoughts are *there*; and we return to the desolate home feeling that all that made life lovely has been left behind on the bleak hillside . . . Yet the spirit now is *free*, and the unseen angel at our side points upwards from the grave and whispers, 'He is not here, but is risen.' The dear one returns with us to our home, ready and able, as never before, to comfort, encourage, and beckon us onward.

William Littleboy

Welcoming a special child

A meeting was held quite far from earth;
It's time again for another birth.
Said the angels to the Lord above,
'This special child will need much love.

He may not run or laugh or play;
His thoughts may seem quite far away.
In many ways he won't adapt,
And he'll be known as handicapped.

So let's be careful where he's sent;
We want his life to be content.
Please, Lord, find parents who
Will do a special job for you.

They will not realise right away
The leading role they're asked to play;
But with this child sent from above
Comes stronger faith and richer love.

And soon they'll know the privilege given
In caring for their gift from heaven;
Their precious charge, so meek and mild,
Is heaven's very special child.'

Edna Massimilla

Starting over – fighting back
And so we must begin to live again
We of the damaged bodies
And assaulted minds.
Starting from scratch with the rubble of our lives
And picking up the dust
of dreams once dreamt.

And we stand there, naked in our vulnerability
Proud of starting over, fighting back
But full of weak humility
At the awesomeness of the task.

We, without a future,
Safe, defined and delivered
Now salute you God,
Knowing that nothing is safe,
Secure, inviolable here
Except you,
And even that eludes our minds at times.

And we hate you
As we love you,
And our anger is as strong
As our pain,
Our grief as deep as oceans
And our need as great as mountains.

So, as we take our first few steps forward
Into the abyss of the future,
We would pray for:
Courage to go places for the first time
And just be there,
Courage to become what we have
Not been before,
And accept it.
And bravery to look deep
Within our souls to find
New ways.

We did not want it easy, God,
But we did not quite contemplate
That it would be this hard
This long, this lonely.

So, if we are to be turned inside out
And upside down
With even our pockets shaken
Just to check what's rattling
and left behind
We pray that you will keep faith with us
And we with you.
Holding our hands as we weep
Giving us strength to continue
And showing us beacons
Along the way
To becoming new.

We are not fighting you God
Even if it feels like it
But we need your help and company,
As we struggle on.
Fighting back,
And starting over.

Anna McKenzie

They all felt awkward and unhappy suddenly because it was a sort of goodbye they were saying, and they didn't want to think about it.

Then Christopher Robin called out, 'Pooh!'

'Yes,' said Pooh.

'When I'm ... when ... Pooh!'

'Yes, Christopher Robin?'

'I'm not going to do nothing anymore.'

'Never again?'

'Well, not so much. They don't let you.'

Pooh waited for him to go on, but he was silent again.

'Yes, Christopher Robin?' said Pooh helpfully.

'Pooh, when I'm ... you know, when I'm not doing Nothing, will you come up here sometimes?'

'Just me?'

'Yes, Pooh.'

'Will you be here too?'

'Yes Pooh, I will be really, I promise I will be, Pooh.'

'That's good,' said Pooh.

'Pooh, promise you won't forget about me, ever. Not even when I'm a hundred.'

'I promise,' he said.

'Pooh, whatever happens, you will understand, won't you?'

A. A. Milne

Death is but *Crossing* the *World*, as Friends do the Seas; they live in one another still.

For they must needs be present, that love and live in that which is *Omnipresent*.

In this Divine Glass, they see Face to Face; and their Converse is *Free*, as well as *Pure*.

This is the Comfort of Friends, that though they may be said to *Die*, yet their Friendship and Society are, in the best Sense, ever present, because *Immortal*.

William Penn

I had thought that your death
Was a waste and a destruction,
A pain of grief hardly to be endured.
I am only beginning to learn
That your life was a gift and a growing
And a loving left with me.
The desperation of death
Destroyed the existence of love,
But the fact of death
Cannot destroy what has been given.
I am learning to look at life again
Instead of your death and your departing.

Marjorie Pizer

If I should die and leave you here awhile,
Be not like others, sore undone, who keep
Long vigils by the silent dust, and weep.
For my sake, turn again to life and smile,
Nerving thy heart and trembling hand to do
Something to comfort weaker hearts than thine,
Complete those dear unfinished tasks of mine,
And I perchance may therein comfort you.

A. Price Hughes

In the pain and fear of giving birth
I watched you come into this world

With awe and wonder in my heart
Then I held you in my arms and cried.

In the pain and fear of impending death
I watched you go out of this world
With shock and disbelief in my heart
Then I held you in my arms and cried.

In the pain and fear of bereavement
I've searched for you in this world
With anguish and grief in my heart
Then I held the memory of you in my arms
and cried . . . and cried.

From Enduring, Sharing, Loving

Water bugs and dragonflies

Down below the surface of a quiet pond lived a little colony of
water bugs. They were a happy colony, living far away from the
sun. For many months they were very busy, scurrying over the soft
mud on the bottom of the pond.

They did notice that every once in a while one of their colony
seemed to lose interest in going about with its friends. Clinging
to the stem of a pond lily, it gradually moved out of sight and was
seen no more.

'Look!' said one of the water bugs to another. 'One of our
colony is climbing up the lily stalk. Where do you suppose she is
going?'

Up, up, up it went slowly. Even as they watched, the water bug
disappeared from sight. Its friends waited and waited but it didn't
return.

'That's funny!' said one water bug to another.

'Wasn't she happy here?' asked a second water bug.

'Where do you suppose she went?' wondered a third.

No one had an answer. They were greatly puzzled.

Finally one of the water bugs, a leader in the colony, gathered its friends together. 'I have an idea. The next one of us who climbs up the lily stalk must promise to come back and tell us where he or she went and why.'

'We promise', they said solemnly.

One spring day, not long after, the very water bug who had suggested the plan found himself climbing up the lily stalk. Up, up, up he went. Before he knew what was happening, he had broken through the surface of the water, and fallen onto the broad, green lily pad above.

When he awoke, he looked about with surprise. He couldn't believe what he saw. A startling change had come to his old body. His movement revealed four silver wings and a long tail. Even as he struggled, he felt an impulse to move his wings. The warmth of the sun soon dried the moisture from the new body. He moved his wings again and suddenly found himself up above the water. He had become a dragonfly.

Swooping and dipping in great curves, he flew through the air. He felt exhilarated in the new atmosphere.

By and by, the new dragonfly lighted happily on a lily pad to rest. Then it was that he chanced to look below to the bottom of the pond. Why, he was right above his old friends, the water bugs! There they were, scurrying about, just as he had been doing some time before.

Then the dragonfly remembered the promise: 'The next one of us who climbs up the lily stalk will come back and tell where he or she went and why.'

Without thinking, the dragonfly darted down. Suddenly he hit the surface of the water and bounced away. Now that he was a dragonfly, he could no longer go into the water.

'I can't return!' he said in dismay. 'At least I tried, but I can't keep my promise. Even if I could go back, not one of the water bugs would know me in my new body. I guess I'll just have to wait until they become dragonflies too. Then they'll understand what happened to me, and where I went.'

And the dragonfly winged off happily into its wonderful new world of sun and air.

A prayer after reading
Water bugs and dragonflies

Thank you, God, for the story of the
water bugs and the dragonflies.
Thank you for the miracle that
makes shiny dragonflies out of ugly bugs.
Please remember N, who
has left the pond we live in. Give
him/her a good life too, in a
wonderful new world of sun and air.
And then remember me, and let
me some day be with him/her.
Amen.

Doris Stickney

'I was not aware of the moment'

I was not aware of the moment when I first crossed the threshold
of this life. What was the power that made me open out into this
vast mystery like a bud in the forest at midnight! When in the
morning I looked upon the light I felt in a moment that I was no
stranger in this world, that the inscrutable without name and form
had taken me in its arms in the form of my own mother. Even
so, in death the same unknown will appear as ever known to me.

Rabindranath Tagore

Some months ago I was asked by a friend to visit a young couple
whose two year old daughter had been found dead in her cot.
They were stunned and haunted by the old question, Why? and,
sometimes, Why her? I simply could not offer them the conven-
tional reassurance about it all being in God's providence, a mystery
now but one day to be seen as part of a loving plan. I know that
many good souls derive lasting comfort from such counsel, and it
certainly squares with a good deal in the Bible, and is to be found
in many books of devotion and pastoral practice. But to me it has

become unconvincing and suggests a picture of God I find impossible to love, arrogant though that sounds. I said to them instead
that their child's death was a tragic accident, an unforeseeable
failure in the functioning of the little body, that, so far from being
willed or planned by God, it was for him a disaster and frustration
of his will for life and fulfilment, just as it was for them, that God
shared their pain and loss and was with them in it. I went on to
say that God is not a potentate ordering this or that to happen,
but that the world is full of chance and accident, and God has let
it be so because that is the one sort of world in which freedom,
development, responsibility and love could come into being, but
that God was committed to this kind of a world in love and to
each person in it, and was with them in this tragedy, giving himself
to them in fortitude, healing and faith to help them through. And
their child was held in that same caring, suffering love.

Bishop John V. Taylor

The bright field

I have seen the sun break through
to illuminate a small field
for a while, and gone my way
and forgotten it. But that was the pearl
of great price, the one field that had treasure in it.
I realise now that I must give all that I have
to possess it. Life is not hurrying
on to a receding future, nor hankering after
an imagined past. It is turning
aside like Moses to see the miracle
of the lit bush, to a brightness
that seemed as transitory as your youth
once, but is the eternity that awaits you.

R. S. Thomas

Roads go ever ever on
Over rock and under tree,
By caves where never sun has shone,
By streams that never find the sea.

Over snow by winter sown,
And through the merry flowers of June,
Over grass and over stone,
And under mountains in the moon.

Roads go ever ever on
Under clouds and under stars,
Yet feet that wandering have gone
Turn at last to home afar.
Eyes that fire and sword have seen
And horror in the halls of stone,
Look at last on meadows green,
And trees and hills they long have known.

J. R. R. Tolkien

All appeared new, and strange at first, inexpressibly rare and delightful and beautiful. I was a little stranger, which at my entrance into the world was saluted and surrounded with innumerable joys. My knowledge was Divine. I knew by intuition those things which since my Apostasy, I collected again by the highest reason. My very ignorance was advantageous. I seemed as one brought into the Estate of Innocence. All things were spotless and pure and glorious: yea, and infinitely mine, and joyful and precious. I knew not that there were any sins, or complaints or laws. I dreamed not of poverties, contentions or vices. All tears and quarrels were hidden from mine eyes. Everything was at rest, free and immortal. I knew nothing of sickness or death or rents or exaction, either for tribute or bread. In the absence of these I was entertained like an Angel with the works of God in their splendour and glory, I saw all in the peace of Eden; Heaven and Earth did sing my Creator's praises, and could not make more melody to Adam, than to me. All Time was Eternity, and a perpetual Sabbath. Is it not strange, that an infant should be heir of the whole World, and see those mysteries which the books of the learned never unfold?

Boys and girls tumbling in the street, and playing, were moving jewels. I knew not that they were born or should die; but all things abided eternally as they were in their proper places. Eternity was manifest in the Light of the Day, and something infinite behind everything appeared: which talked with my expectation and moved my desire. The city seemed to stand in Eden, or to be built in Heaven. The streets were mine, the temple was mine, the people were mine, their clothes and gold and silver were mine, as much as their sparkling eyes, fair skins and ruddy faces. The skies were mine, and so were the sun and moon and stars, and all the World was mine; and I the only spectator and enjoyer of it. I knew no churlish properties nor bounds, nor divisions: but all properties and divisions were mine: all treasures and possessors of them. So that with much ado I was corrupted, and made to learn the dirty devices of this world. Which now I unlearn, and become, as it were, a little child again that I may enter into the Kingdom of God.

Thomas Traherne

Mary Poppins had gone. Jane read the note she had left.

'Mrs Brill!' she called. 'What does "Au Revoir" mean?'

'I think, Miss Jane dear, it means "To meet again".'

Jane and Michael looked at each other. Joy and understanding shone in their eyes. They knew what Mary Poppins meant.

Michael gave a long sigh of relief. 'That's all right,' he said shakily. 'She always does what she says she will.'

He turned away.

'Michael, are you crying?' Jane asked.

He twisted his head and tried to smile at her.

'No I'm not,' he said. 'It is only my eyes.'

P. L. Travers

The artist chooses, let us say, a certain size of canvas as suitable for a certain theme. But, as he works, this formal requirement, which he himself has willed, imposes a discipline upon his creativity. He is faced with the problem of working within his self-chosen form; and the solution to the problem must be worked out of the creative process. The problem arises not because the artist has chosen the 'wrong' form but because he has chosen *some kind* of form – because he has chosen not merely to express himself but to do so in some kind of determinate way. This problem is present in all creativity, in every process of imparting oneself to that which is truly other than oneself: one must 'find the way' in which, through risk and failure and the redemption of failure, the other may be able to receive.

In the second place, the principle does not imply that evil is willed by the Creator, either for its own sake or as a means to a greater good. The artist does not will the moment of lost control, nor intend it as a means to the completion and the greatness of his work. He does not will the demand which that moment makes upon him – the demand to redeem it and to save his work. He does not will the problem of creativity: his will is to overcome the problem in every particular form and moment in which it may arise. Each problematical moment is unforeseen and unforeseeable: it arises because the object of creation is truly an other. The demand on the artist is to overcome the unforeseeable problem – to handle it in such a way that it becomes a new and unforeseen richness in his work. The artist fails not when he confronts a problem but when he abandons it: and he proves his greatness when he leaves no problem abandoned. Our faith in the Creator is that he leaves no problem abandoned and no evil unredeemed.

We do not believe, of the children who died at Aberfan, that God willed their death as a means to some greater good. If we so believed, we would find that alleged 'good' tainted, compromised and unacceptable: like Ivan Karamazov, we would have no part in it and would 'hand in our ticket'. We believe that, at the moment when the mountain of Aberfan slipped, 'something went wrong': the step of creative risk was the step of disaster: the creative process passed out of control. Our faith is in a Creator who does not abandon even this, nor those who suffered, wept and died in it, but Who so gives of Himself that He finds, for the redeeming of this, yet more to give, and knows no respite until the slag-heap has become a fair hillside, and the hearts of the parents have been enlarged by sorrow, and the children themselves understand and are glad to have so feared and wept and died. Our preaching on the Sunday after the tragedy was not of a God Who, from the top of the mountain, caused or permitted, for His own inscrutable reasons, its disruption and descent: but of one who received, at the foot of the mountain, its appalling impact, and Who, in the extremity of endeavour, will find yet new resource to restore and redeem.

W. H. Vanstone

God gives life,
And God takes life away
And the taking away is so terribly painful,
Because what he gives is so very good.

Lindon Jane Vogel

Our birth is but a sleep and a forgetting:
The Soul that rises with us, our life's Star
　　Hath had elsewhere its setting,
　　　And cometh from afar:
　　Not in entire forgetfulness,
　　And not in utter nakedness,
But trailing clouds of glory do we come
　　From God, who is our home:
Heaven lies about us in our infancy!

William Wordsworth

The journey

They had been travelling together for some time – a little group on a special journey. They each had a tent in which to live – and their tents were of different shapes and sizes – each having its own unique character and individual beauty. Each day the group pitched their tents a little nearer to their destination – a place they could not see – but which was going to hold for them more than all the experiences of the journey put together.

The group had begun with two people – or perhaps I should say three – since when they had lived on their own in the open countryside, the two, at different times, had met the Master of the Journey. He had pointed them in the direction of the destination, and from the day of this meeting he went with each of them on the journey. When on the way these two met each other, they decided to pitch their tents together. Three more soon joined their group and from then on their five tents were pitched side by side.

A time came when the tent of one of the first two began to be a problem for him and the journey became difficult. Some work was done to try and mend his tent but there was little improvement, and the fabric of his tent seemed to be wearing out. The others in the group talked to the Master of the Journey about the situation. They knew that he was able to restore worn out tents and that he loved them all very much. The Master knew that it was best for the group not to tell them all his plans at once, so they continued their journey with him, wondering what the future would hold. As time passed the failing tent became more and more difficult to live in, and the one who lived there needed a new living-place free from the suffering of the tent. It was not that he minded the journey – in fact he loved travelling with the rest of the group – but he knew that what awaited them at the end of the journey was something to look forward to very much.

One morning something very special happened. The one whose tent had now got to the point when it was becoming impossible to live in, looked out – and saw that instead of being on open ground (as his tent had been throughout the journey) it was inside a magnificent house. The room was set out in a way that perfectly suited him and he felt very much at home. From inside his tent he saw standing in the room his greatest friend – the Master of the Journey. He could now see him in a way he never had before. He realized that now inside the house he did not need the tent any longer. The Master of the Journey reached out his hand to him and he went quietly from his tent into his own room in the Master's home. What joy to be there with him!

The one whose tent had been pitched next to his since they joined together did not see the room, or the house, or the Master. These are all invisible to those who are still on the journey. All that was there to be seen was that the tent was now empty and the one whose tent it had been was no longer there. The group knew where he had gone – his journey was over – he had arrived at the Master's home. With his own special room there he had no more need of the tent.

It was difficult for the group to know how to think about the tent now. In one way it was very special as it had been the tent in which the one they loved had always lived. Yet the tent was not the person – and now that he was no longer visible to them, the tent was only worn out fabric which was no longer needed. The tent was carefully packed away; and the group along with many friends who were also heading for the same destination as they were, got together to say, 'Thank You' to the Master of the Journey for giving them such a lovely person and to rejoice together that the Master of the Journey loved them all so much and that he was guiding them all towards the enjoyment of his home.

The little group then continued their journey together. It was strange for them as they moved on with their tents no longer to have beside theirs the tent of the one who meant so much to them. But in some ways it was as if he was with them as he had always been, because there was much that was lovely in each of them, and in the life of their group, which came from the love he had given each of them and the special way he had cared for them all.

Graeme C. Young

The Long Silence

At the end of time, billions of people were scattered on a great plain before God's throne. Most shrank back from the brilliant light before them.

But some groups near the front talked heatedly not with cringing shame, but with belligerence.

'Can God judge us? How can He know about suffering?' snapped a pert young brunette. She ripped open a sleeve to reveal a tattooed number from a Nazi concentration camp. 'We endured terror . . . beatings . . . torture . . . death!'

In another group a Negro boy lowered his collar.

'What about this?' he demanded, showing an ugly rope burn. 'Lynched for no crime but being black!'

In another crowd, a pregnant schoolgirl with sullen eyes, 'Why should I suffer?' she murmured. 'It wasn't my fault.' Far out across the plain were hundreds of such groups. Each had a complaint against God for the evil and suffering He permitted in His world.

How lucky God was to live in Heaven where all was sweetness and Light, where there was no weeping or fear, no hunger or hatred. What did God know of all that man had been forced to endure in this world. For God leads a pretty sheltered life, they said.

So each of these groups sent forth their leader, chosen because he had suffered the most. A Jew, a Negro, a person from Hiroshima, a horribly deformed arthritic, a thalidomide child. In the centre of the plain they consulted with each other. At last they were ready to present their case. It was rather clever.

Before God could be qualified to be their judge, He must endure what they had endured. Their decision was that God should be sentenced to live on earth – as a man!

Let him be born a Jew. Let the legitimacy of his birth be doubted. Give him a work so difficult that even his family will think him out of his mind when he tries to do it. Let him be betrayed by his closest friends. Let him face false charges, be tried by a prejudiced jury and convicted by a cowardly judge. Let him be tortured.

At last, let him see what it means to be terribly alone. Then let him die. Let him die so that there can be no doubt he died. Let there be a great host of witnesses to verify it.

As each leader announced his portion of the sentence, loud

murmurs of approval went up from the throng of people assembled.

When the last had finished pronouncing sentence, there was a long silence. No one uttered another word. No one moved. For suddenly all knew that God had already served His sentence.

Source unknown

Stations

(A story about Thomas the Train and a little bear named Bradley)

Bradley and his family lived in a beautiful house that had big tall trees all around. Bradley was getting ready for a trip. He didn't know where he was going but he knew that he was going to ride with his friend Thomas the Train. Now Thomas, in his life, had taken people from all over to different places. He always got them to where they needed to go safe and sound. Once on the train, Thomas took care of everything. There were bears on the train to help Thomas do his job. Some bears looked after bears; some bears played with bears. Bears were of every age and came from all over the world. No one was ever sick on the train; even those bears who were sick before weren't sick anymore. Every type of food – good stuff and junk stuff – was available twenty-four hours a day. There were special things on Thomas for little bears – lots of toys and a big playground like Disneyland. Little bears always got special treatment on Thomas because sometimes they travel alone. Thomas and the bears on the train that helped Thomas kept a special eye on little bears so that they were never lonely.

Soon Bradley was ready to go to the train station where Thomas was meeting him. Bradley's family took Bradley to the train station. They were sad and worried because he was such a little bear to be travelling on his own. But they knew and trusted Thomas because Thomas had been doing this job for a long time. They knew Thomas would take good care of Bradley and make sure he arrived safely to meet his family at the next train station.

Bradley hugged his family a temporary good-bye because Thomas promised to get Bradley to the next station where his family would meet him. It was still very very hard to say goodbye because Bradley wanted his family to come and they wanted to come with Bradley. But this was a trip that Bradley had to take by himself and his family had lots of other things to do before they met Bradley at the next station. Bradley and his family promised to think about each other often and to remember all the special memories and times they had together. Thomas promised the family that he would take extra good care of Bradley, just as Bradley's family promised Thomas that they would take good care of each other. Lots of friends and family were there to wave Bradley off and the family and friends also promised to take good care of each other and Bradley's family.

As they cried and waved at Bradley on Thomas, they saw a rainbow. Someone said, a long time ago, that a rainbow is a promise waiting to happen and that a rainbow will always be over little Bradley until he sees his family at the next station and then they would travel the rest of the journey together forever.

The End

Source unknown

Do not stand at my grave and weep
I am not there. I do not sleep.
I am a thousand winds that blow.
I am the diamond glints on snow.
I am the sunlight on ripened grain,
I am the gentle autumn rain.
When you awaken in the morning's hush
I am the swift uplifting rush
Of quiet birds in circled flight.
I am the soft stars that shine at night.
Do not stand at my grave and cry,
I am not there; I did not die.

Anonymous, left by Stephen Cummins,
a soldier killed in Northern Ireland

I have seen death too often to believe in death.
It is not an ending, but a withdrawal.
As one who finishes a long journey,
   Stills the motor,
   Turns off the lights,
   Steps from the car,
And walks up the path
To the home that awaits him.

Source unknown

God's lent child

I'll lend you for a little time
A child of Mine, God said,
for you to love the while she lives
And mourn for when she's dead.

It may be six or seven weeks,
Or thirteen years, or three,
But will you, till I call her back,
Take care of her for Me?

She'll bring her charm to gladden you
And should her stay be brief,
You'll have her lovely memories
As solace for your grief.

I cannot promise she will stay,
Since all from Earth return,
But there are lessons taught down 'there'
I want this child to learn.

And there, with you on Earth
This child of mine I lend,
For many souls that she will touch,
With the lessons that I send.

I looked the wide world over
In my search for people true,
And from the throngs who crowd life's way,
I have selected you.

Now will you give her all your love,
Nor think the labour vain,
Nor hate Me when I call around
To take her back again?

I fancy that I hear you say,
'Dear Lord, Thy will be done',
For all the joy this child has brought,
All fateful risks we run.

We sheltered her with tenderness,
We love her while we may,
And for the happiness we've known,
We shall forever grateful stay.

But You came round to call for her
Much sooner than we'd planned –
Dear Lord, forgive this grief,
And help us understand.

Author unknown

You are very special

In all the world there is nobody, nobody like you. Since the
beginning of time there has never been another person like you.
Nobody has your smile, your eyes, your hands, your hair. Nobody
owns your handwriting, your voice. You're Special.

Nobody can paint your brush strokes. Nobody had your taste
for food or music or dance or art. Nobody in the universe sees
things as you do. In all time there has never been anyone who
laughs in exactly your way, and what makes you laugh or cry or

think may have a totally different response in another. So You're Special.

You're different from any other person who has ever lived in the history of the Universe. You are the only one in the whole creation who has your particular set of abilities. There is always someone who is better at one thing or another. Every person is your superior in at least one way. Nobody in the universe can reach the quality of the combination of your talents, your feelings; like a roomful of musical instruments, some might excel in one way or another but nobody can match the symphonic sound when all are played together. Your Symphony. Through all eternity no one will ever walk, talk, think or do exactly like you. You're Special.

You're rare and in all rarity there is enormous value and because of your great value the need for you to imitate anyone else is absolutely wrong. You're Special and it is no accident you are. Please realise that God made you for a special purpose. He has a job for you to do that nobody else can do as well as you can. Out of billions of applicants only one is qualified. Only one has the unique and right combination of what it takes and that one is You.

You're Special.

Source unknown

One night I had a dream.
I dreamed I was walking along the beach with the Lord, and across the sky flashed scenes from my life.
For each scene, I noticed two sets of footprints in the sand;
One belonged to me, the other to the Lord.
When the last scene of my life flashed before me,
I looked back at the footprints in the sand.
I noticed that many times along the path of life,
there was only one set of footprints.
I noticed that it happened at the very lowest and saddest times in my life.
This really bothered me and I questioned the Lord about it:

'Lord, You said that once I decided to follow You,
You would walk with me all the way.
But I have noticed that during the most troublesome times in
my life, there is only one set of footprints. I don't understand
why in times when I needed You most, You would leave me.'
The Lord replied:
'My precious, precious child, I love you and would never,
never leave you during your times of trial and suffering.
When you see only one set of footprints –
It was then that I carried you.'

Anonymous

. . . the deceased has removed into a better country, and bounded
away to a happier inheritance; . . . thou hast not lost thy son, but
bestowed him henceforth in an inviolable spot. Say not then, I
pray thee, I am no longer called 'father', for why art thou no
longer called so, when thy son abideth? For surely thou didst not
part with my child, nor lose thy son? Rather thou hast gotten
him, and hast him in greater safety. Wherefore, no longer shalt
thou be called 'father' here only, but also in heaven; so that thou
hast not lost the title 'father' here only, but hast gained it in a
nobler sense; for henceforth thou shalt be called father not of
a mortal child, but of an immortal . . . For think not, because he
is not present, that therefore he is lost; for had he been absent in
a foreign land, the title of thy relationship had not gone from thee
with his body.

Source unknown

There are no dead people
There are only the living,
On earth and beyond.
Death is real,
But it's nothing but a moment,
A second, a step.
The step from provisional to permanent,

From temporal to eternal.
So in the death of the child, the adolescent is born,
From the caterpillar emerges the butterfly.
From the grain, the full-blown ear.

Source unknown

They are not lost, our dearest loves,
Nor have they travelled far,
Just stepped inside home's loveliest room,
And left the door ajar . . .

Source unknown

They said on his first day on earth,
Better far if he'd died at birth.
How could they know.
How could they tell the joy he'd bring,
He taught our hearts the way to sing,
We loved him so.

We learned together through the years
To show the joy, but hide the tears,
They must not see.
They'd never learn the hurt they caused
Through thoughtless stares that on him paused
So carelessly.

And as he grew, we never grieved
To see how little he achieved,
No praise he'd lose.
His progress made in life's tough school
We measured with a shorter rule
Than scholars use.

I can't believe he owed his day
To some genetic disarray

Wrongly conceived.
He came into this world, and there
He lived to teach us how to care.
This he achieved.

Anonymous

Think . . .
Of stepping on shore, and finding it heaven.
Of taking hold of a hand, and finding it God's hand.
Of breathing a new air, and finding it celestial air.
Of feeling invigorated, and finding it immortality.
Of passing from storm and tempest to an unbroken calm.
Of waking up and, and finding it Home.

Anonymous

Hymns and Songs

(These are set out in alphabetical order of first lines.)

1   All my hope on God is founded;
         He doth still my trust renew.
      Me through change and chance he guideth,
         Only good and only true.
            God unknown,
            He alone
      Calls my heart to be his own.

2   Pride of man and earthly glory,
         Sword and crown betray his trust;
      What with care and toil he buildeth,
         Tower and temple, fall to dust.
            But God's power,
            Hour by hour,
      Is my temple and my tower.

3   God's great goodness ay endureth,
         Deep his wisdom, passing thought:
      Splendour, light, and life attend him,
         Beauty springeth out of nought.
            Evermore,
            From his store
      New-born worlds rise and adore.

4   Daily doth the almighty giver
         Bounteous gifts on us bestow;
      His desire our soul delighteth,

Pleasure leads us where we go.
Love doth stand
At his hand;
Joy doth wait on his command.

5   Still from man to God eternal
Sacrifice of praise be done,
High above all praises praising
For the gift of Christ his Son.
Christ doth call
One and all:
Ye who follow shall not fall

Robert Bridges (1844–1930), after Joachim Neander (1650–1680)

All things bright and beautiful,
all creatures great and small,
all things wise and wonderful,
the Lord God made them all.

Each little flower that opens,
each little bird that sings,
he made their glowing colours,
he made their tiny wings.
All things bright and beautiful etc.

The purple headed mountain,
the river running by,
the sunset and the morning
that brightens up the sky.
All things bright and beautiful etc.

The cold wind in the winter,
the pleasant summer sun,
the ripe fruits in the garden,
he made them every one.
All things bright and beautiful etc.

The tall trees in the greenwood,
the meadows for our play,
the rushes by the water,
to gather every day.
All things bright and beautiful etc.

Mrs C. F. Alexander (1818–1895)

Amazing grace! How sweet the sound
That saved a wretch like me.
I once was lost, but now am found.
Was blind, but now I see.

'Twas grace that taught my heart to fear,
And grace my fears relieved.
How precious did that grace appear
The hour I first believed.

Through many dangers, toils and snares,
I have already come;
'Tis grace that brought me safe thus far;
And grace will lead me home.

When we've been there ten thousand years,
Bright shining as the sun,
We've no less days to sing God's praise
Than when we've first begun.

John Newton (1725–1807)

Be still, for the presence of the Lord, the Holy One is here.
Come bow before him now, with reverence and fear.
In Him no sin is found, we stand on Holy ground.
Be still, for the presence of the Lord, the Holy One is here.

Be still, for the glory of the Lord is shining all around;
He burns with holy fire, with splendour he is crowned.
How awesome is the sight, our radiant King of light!
Be still, for the glory of the Lord is shining all around.

Be still, for the power of the Lord is moving in this place,
He comes to cleanse and heal, to minister his grace.
No work too hard for Him, in faith receive from him;
Be still, for the power of the Lord is moving in this place.

David J. Evans

Be thou my vision, O Lord of my heart,
be all else but nought to me, save that thou art;
   be thou my best thought in the day and the night,
   both waking and sleeping, thy presence my light.

Be thou my wisdom, be thou my true word,
be thou ever with me, and I with thee, Lord;
   be thou my great Father, and I thy true son;
   be thou in me dwelling, and I with thee one.

Riches I heed not, nor man's empty praise:
be thou mine inheritance now and always;
   be thou and thou only the first in my heart;
   O Sovereign of heaven, my treasure thou art.

High King of heaven, thou heaven's bright Sun,
O grant me its joys after vict'ry is won;
   great Heart of my own heart, whatever befall,
   still be thou my vision, O Ruler of all.

Ancient Irish
tr. by Mary Elizabeth Byrne (1880–1931)
Versified by Eleanor Henrietta Hull (1860–1935)

Bind us together Lord,
Bind us together with cords that cannot be broken;
Bind us together Lord,
O bind us together in love!

There is only one God,
There is only one King,
There is only one Body
That is why we sing:

Bind us together . . .

God has many gifts
Given by his Son
Building the Body of Christ
Creating a faith that is one;

Bind us together . . .

We are the family of God,
Joined by the Spirit above,
Working together with Christ
Growing and building in love;

Bind us together . . .

Bob Gillman

Colours of day
dawn into the mind,
the sun has come up,
the night is behind.
Go down in the city,
into the street,
and let's give the message
to the people we meet.

So light up the fire
and let the flame burn,
open the door, let Jesus return.
Take seeds of his Spirit,
let the fruit grow,
tell the people of Jesus, let his love show.

Go through the park,
on into the town;
the sun still shines on
it never goes down.
The light of the world
is risen again;
the people of darkness
are needing our friend.

Open your eyes
look into the sky,
the darkness has come,
the sun came to die.
The evening draws on,
the sun disappears,
but Jesus is living,
and his Spirit is near.

Sue McClellan, John Paculabo and Keith Rycroft

1 Dear Lord and Father of mankind,
   forgive our foolish ways;
   re-clothe us in our rightful mind;
   in purer lives Thy service find,
   in deeper reverence, praise.

2 In simple trust like theirs who heard,
   beside the Syrian sea,
   the gracious calling of the Lord,

let us, like them, without a word
rise up and follow Thee.

3   O Sabbath rest by Galilee!
O calm of hills above,
where Jesus knelt to share with Thee
the silence of eternity,
interpreted by love!

4   With that deep hush subduing all
our words and works that drown
the tender whisper of Thy call,
as noiseless let Thy blessing fall,
as fell Thy manna down.

5   Drop Thy still dews of quietness,
till all our strivings cease;
take from our souls the strain and stress,
and let our ordered lives confess
the beauty of Thy peace.

6   Breathe through the heats of our desire
Thy coolness and Thy balm;
let sense be dumb, let flesh retire;
speak through the earthquake, wind, and fire,
O still small voice of calm!

John Greenleaf Whittier (1807–1882)

Do not be worried and upset.
Believe in God, believe also in me,
There are many rooms in my Father's house,
And I'm going to prepare a place,
Prepare a place for you.

I am the way, the truth and the life;
No one goes to the Father except by me.

I am the way, the truth and the life,
And I'm going to prepare a place,
Prepare a place for you.

After I go and prepare a place for you,
I will come back and take you to myself,
So that you may come and be where I am.
And I'm going to prepare a place,
Prepare a place for you.

I am the way, the truth and the life;
No one goes to the Father except by me.
I am the way, the truth and the life,
And I'm going to prepare a place,
Prepare a place for you.
And I'm going to prepare a place,
Prepare a place for you.

From Sing Good News

Fleetingly known, yet ever remembered,
These are our children now and always:
These whom we see not we will forget not,
Morning and evening all of our days.

Lives that touched our lives, tenderly, briefly,
Now in the one light living always:
Names in our hearts now, safe from all harm now,
We will remember all of our days.

As we recall them, silently name them,
Open our hearts, Lord, now and always:
Grant to us, grieving, love for the living;
Strength for each other all of our days.

Safe in your peace, Lord, hold these our children;
Grace, light and laughter grant them each day:

Cherish and hold them till we may know them
When to your glory we find our way.

SANDS (Stillbirth and Neonatal Death Society)
(May be sung to the tune 'Morning has broken')

Give me oil in my lamp
Give me oil in my lamp, keep me burning,
Give me oil in my lamp, I pray.
Give me oil in my lamp, keep me burning,
Keep me burning till the break of day.

Chorus:
Sing Hosanna! Sing Hosanna! Sing Hosanna to the King of
* Kings!*
Sing Hosanna! Sing Hosanna! Sing Hosanna to the King!

Give me joy in my heart, keep me singing,
Give me joy in my heart, I pray,
Give me joy in my heart, keep me singing,
Keep me singing till the break of day.

Give me love in my heart, keep me serving,
Give me love in my heart, I pray.
Give me love in my heart, keep me serving,
Keep me serving till the break of day.

Give me peace in my heart, keep me resting,
Give me peace in my heart, I pray.
Give me peace in my heart, keep me resting
Keep me resting till the break of day.

Anonymous

God be in my head and in my understanding;
God be in my eyes, and in my looking;
God be in my mouth, and in my speaking;

God be in my heart, and in my thinking;
God be at mine end, and my departing.

Horae BVM Sarum (1514)

He who would valiant be,
'Gainst all disaster,
Let him in constancy
Follow the Master,
There's no discouragement
Shall make him first relent
His first avowed intent
To be a pilgrim.

Whoso beset him round
With dismal stories,
Do but themselves confound –
His strength the more is.
No foes shall stay his might,
Though he with giants fight:
He will make good his right
To be a pilgrim.

Since, Lord, thou dost defend
Us with thy Spirit,
We know we at the end
Shall life inherit.
Then fancies flee away!
I'll fear not what men say,
I'll labour night and day
To be a pilgrim.

Percy Dearmer (1867–1936) after John Bunyan

I danced in the morning
when the world was begun,
and I danced in the moon

and the stars and the sun,
and I came down from heaven
and I danced on the earth;
at Bethlehem
I had my birth:

Dance, then, wherever you may be;
I am the Lord of the Dance, said he,
and I'll lead you all wherever you may be,
and I'll lead you all in the dance, said he.

I danced for the scribe
and the pharisee,
but they would not dance
and they wouldn't follow me;
I danced for the fishermen,
for James and John;
they came with me
and the dance went on:

I danced on the Sabbath
and I cured the lame;
the holy people
said it was a shame.
They whipped and they stripped
and they hung me high
and they left me there
on the cross to die:

I danced on a Friday
when the sky turned black;
it's hard to dance
with the devil on your back.
They buried my body
and they thought I'd gone;
but I am the dance
and I still go on:

They cut me down
and I leap up high;
I am the life
that'll never, never die;
I'll live in you
if you'll live in me:
I am the Lord
of the Dance, said he:

Dance, then, wherever you may be;
I am the Lord of the Dance, said he,
and I'll lead you all wherever you may be,
and I'll lead you all in the dance, said he.

Sydney Carter

If I were a butterfly

1   If I were a butterfly,
      I'd thank you, Lord, for giving me wings.
    And if I were a robin in a tree,
      I'd thank you, Lord, that I could sing.
    And if I were a fish in the sea,
      I'd wiggle my tail and I'd giggle with glee,
    But I just thank you, Father, for making me 'me'.

Refrain
For you gave me a heart and you gave me a smile.
You gave me Jesus and you made me your child.
And I just thank you, Father, for making me 'me'.

2   If I were an elephant,
      I'd thank you, Lord, by raising my trunk,
    And if I were a kangaroo,
      You know I'd hop right up to you,
    And if I were an octopus,
      I'd thank you, Lord, for my fine looks,
    But I just thank you, Father, for making me 'me'.

3 If I were a wiggly worm,
    I'd thank you, Lord, that I could squirm.
And if I were a billy goat
    I'd thank you Lord for my strong throat,
And if I were a fuzzy-wuzzy bear,
    I'd thank you, Lord, for my fuzzy-wuzzy hair,
But I just thank you, Father, for making me 'me'.

Brian Howard

Jesus, friend of little children,
Be a friend to me;
Take my hand, and ever keep me
Close to thee.

Teach me how to grow in goodness,
Daily as I grow:
Thou hast been a child, and surely
Thou dost know.

Never leave me, nor forsake me;
Ever be my friend;
For I need thee, from life's dawning
To its end.

Walter J. Mathams (1853–1931)

1 Jesus lives! thy terrors now
    can, O death, no more appal us;
   Jesus lives! by this we know,
    thou, O grave, canst not enthral us.
      Hallelujah!

2 Jesus lives! henceforth is death
    but the gate of life immortal;
   this shall calm our trembling breath,

when we pass its gloomy portal.
  Hallelujah!

3   Jesus lives! for us He died;
    then, alone to Jesus living,
    pure in heart may we abide,
    glory to our Saviour giving.
      Hallelujah!

4   Jesus lives! our hearts know well,
    naught from us His love shall sever;
    life, nor death, nor powers of hell,
    tear us from His keeping ever.
      Hallelujah!

5   Jesus lives! to Him the throne
    over all the world is given:
    may we go where He is gone,
    rest and reign with Him in heaven.
      Hallelujah!

Christian F. Gellert (1715–1769),
tr. Frances Elizabeth Cox (1812–1897)

Kum Ba Yah

Kum ba yah, my Lord, kum ba yah.
Kum ba yah, my Lord, kum ba yah.
Kum ba yah, my Lord, kum ba yah.
O Lord, kum ba yah.

Someone's crying Lord, kum ba yah.
Someone's crying Lord, kum ba yah.
Someone's crying Lord, kum ba yah.
O Lord, kum ba yah.

Someone's singing Lord, kum ba yah.
Someone's singing Lord, kum ba yah.

Someone's singing Lord, kum ba yah.
O Lord, kum ba yah.

Someone's praying Lord, kum ba yah.
Someone's praying Lord, kum ba yah.
Someone's praying Lord, kum ba yah.
O Lord, kum ba yah.

Hear our prayer, O Lord, hear our prayer.
Keep our friends, O Lord, in your care.
Keep our friends, O Lord, in your care.
O Lord, kum ba yah.

Traditional

Lord of all hopefulness, Lord of all joy,
Whose trust, ever child-like, no cares could destroy,
Be there at our waking, and give us, we pray,
Your bliss in our hearts, Lord, at the break of the day.

Lord of all eagerness, Lord of all faith,
Whose strong hands were skilled at the plane and the lathe,
Be there at our labours, and give us, we pray,
Your strength in our hearts, Lord, at the noon of the day.

Lord of all kindliness, Lord of all grace,
Your hands swift to welcome, your arms to embrace,
Be there at our homing, and give us, we pray,
Your love in our hearts, Lord, at the eve of the day.

Lord of all gentleness, Lord of all calm,
Whose voice is contentment, whose presence is balm,
Be there at our sleeping, and give us, we pray,
Your peace in our hearts, Lord, at the end of the day.

Jan Struther (1901–1953)

Lord, the light of your love is shining,
In the midst of the darkness, shining:
Jesus, light of the world, shine upon us;
Set us free by the truth you now bring us –
Shine on me, shine on me.

Shine, Jesus, shine,
Fill this land with the Father's glory;
Blaze, Spirit, blaze,
Set our hearts on fire.
Flow, river, flow,
Flood the nations with grace and mercy;
Send forth your word,
Lord, and let there be light!

Lord, I come to your awesome presence,
From the shadows into your radiance;
By your blood I may enter your brightness:
Search me, try me, consume all my darkness –
Shine on me, shine on me.

As we gaze on your kingly brightness
So our faces display your likeness,
Ever changing from glory to glory:
Mirrored here may our lives tell your story –
Shine on me, shine on me.

Graham Kendrick

Love Divine, all loves excelling,
Joy of heaven, to earth come down,
Fix in us thy humble dwelling,
All thy faithful mercies crown.
Jesu, thou art all compassion,
Pure unbounded love thou art;
Visit us with thy salvation,
Enter every trembling heart.

Come, almighty to deliver,
Let us all thy life receive;
Suddenly return, and never,
Never more thy temples leave.
Thee we would be always blessing,
Serve thee as thy host above,
Pray, and praise thee, without ceasing,
Glory in thy perfect love.

Finish then thy new creation,
Pure and spotless let us be;
Let us see thy great salvation,
Perfectly restored in thee,
Changed from glory into glory,
Till in heaven we take our place,
Till we cast our crowns before thee,
Lost in wonder, love and praise!

Charles Wesley (1707–1788)

Make me a channel of your peace.
Where there is hatred let me bring your love;
Where there is injury, your pardon, Lord;
And where there's doubt, true faith in you.

O, Master, grant that I may never seek
So much to be consoled as to console;
To be understood as to understand;
To be loved, as to love with all my soul.

Make me a channel of your peace.
Where there's despair in life let me bring hope;
Where there is darkness, only light;
And where there's sadness, ever joy.

O Master, grant that I may never seek
So much to be consoled as to console;

To be understood as to understand;
To be loved, as to love with all my soul.

Make me a channel of your peace.
It is in pardoning that we are pardoned,
In giving to all men that we receive;
And in dying that we are born to eternal life.

Prayer of St Francis

A hymn to the Creator
Morning glory, starlit sky,
Leaves in springtime, swallows' flight,
Autumn gales, tremendous seas,
Sounds and scents of summer night;

Soaring music, tow'ring words,
Art's perfection, scholar's truth,
Joy supreme of human love,
Memory's treasure, grace of youth;

Open, Lord, are these, Thy gifts,
Gifts of love to mind and sense;
Hidden is love's agony,
Love's endeavour, love's expense.

Love that gives gives ever more,
Gives with zeal, with eager hands,
Spares not, keeps not, all outpours,
Ventures all, its all expends.

Drained is love in making full;
Bound in setting others free;
Poor in making many rich;
Weak, in giving power to be.

Therefore He Who Thee reveals
Hangs, O Father, on that Tree
Helpless; and the nails and thorns
Tell of what Thy love must be.

Thou art God; no monarch Thou
Thron'd in easy state to reign;
Thou art God, Whose arms of love
Aching, spent, the world sustain.

W. H. Vanstone

Morning has broken
like the first morning,
blackbird has spoken
like the first bird.
Praise for the singing!
Praise for the morning,
Praise for them, springing
fresh from the Word!

Sweet the rain's new fall,
sunlit from heaven,
like the first dewfall
on the first grass.
Praise for the sweetness
of the wet garden,
sprung in completeness
where his feet pass.

Mine is the sunlight!
Mine is the morning
born of the one light
Eden saw play!
Praise with elation,
Praise every morning,

God's re-creation
of the new day.

Eleanor Farjeon

1   My song is love unknown:
    My Saviour's love to me:
    Love to the loveless shown,
    That they may lovely be.
        O who am I,
            That for my sake,
            My Lord should take
        Frail flesh, and die?

2   He came from His blest Throne,
    Salvation to bestow:
    But men made strange, and none
    The longed-for Christ would know.
        But O my friend!
            My Friend indeed,
            Who at my need
        His life did spend.

3   Sometimes they strew His way,
    And His sweet praises sing;
    Resounding all the day,
    Hosannas to their King.
        Then: Crucify!
            Is all their breath,
            And for His death
        They thirst and cry.

4   Why, what hath my Lord done?
    What makes this rage and spite?
    He made the lame to run,
    He gave the blind their sight.
        Sweet injuries!

Yet they at these
Themselves displease,
And 'gainst Him rise.

5   They rise and needs will have
My dear Lord made away;
A murderer they save;
The Prince of life they slay.
Yet cheerful He
To suffering goes,
That He His foes
From thence might free.

6   In life, no house, no home
My Lord on earth might have;
In death, no friendly tomb
But what a stranger gave.
What may I say?
Heav'n was His home;
But mine the tomb
Wherein He lay.

7   Here might I stay and sing,
No story so divine;
Never was love, dear King,
Never was grief like Thine.
This is my Friend,
In whose sweet praise
I all my days
Could gladly spend.

Samuel Crossman (c. 1624–1683)

Now thank we all our God,
With heart and hands and voices,
Who wondrous things hath done,
In whom his world rejoices;

Who from our mother's arms
   Hath blessed us on our way
With countless gifts of love,
   And still is ours today.

O may this bounteous God
   Through all our life be near us,
With ever joyful hearts
   And blessed peace to cheer us;
And keep us in his grace,
   And guide us when perplexed,
And free us from all ills
   In this world and the next.

All praise and thanks to God
   The Father now be given,
The Son and him who reigns
   With them in highest heaven,
The one eternal God,
   Whom earth and heaven adore;
For thus it was, is now,
   And shall be evermore.

Martin Rinkart (1586–1649),
tr. Catherine Winkworth (1829–1878)

Now the green blade riseth from the buried grain,
Wheat that in dark earth many days has lain;
Love lives again, that with the dead has been:
Love is come again,
Like wheat that springeth green.

In the grave they laid him, Love whom men had slain,
Thinking that never he would wake again,
Laid in the earth like grain that sleeps unseen:
Love is come again,
Like wheat that springeth green.

Forth he came at Easter, like the risen grain,
He that for three days in the grave had lain,
Quick from the dead my risen Lord is seen:
Love is come again,
Like wheat that springeth green.

When our hearts are wintry, grieving or in pain,
Thy touch can call us back to life again,
Fields of our hearts that dead and bare have been:
Love is come again,
Like wheat that springeth green.

J. M. C. Crum

Caribbean Lord's Prayer

Our Father who is in heaven.
Hallowed be your name.
Your Kingdom come, your will be done,
Hallowed be your name.

On earth as it is in heaven,
Hallowed be your name.
Give us this day our daily bread,
Hallowed be your name.

Forgive us all our trespasses,
Hallowed be your name.
As we forgive those who trespass against us,
Hallowed be your name.

And lead us not into temptation,
Hallowed be your name.
But deliver us from all that is evil,
Hallowed be your name.

For Yours is the Kingdom, the Power and the Glory,
Hallowed be your name.

For ever and for ever and ever.
Hallowed be your name.

Amen, Amen, it shall be so,
Hallowed be your name.
Amen, Amen, it shall be so,
Hallowed be your name.

The Lord's my Shepherd, I'll not want;
   he makes me down to lie
in pastures green; he leadeth me
   the quiet waters by.

My soul he doth restore again,
   and me to walk doth make
within the paths of righteousness,
   e'en for his own name's sake.

Yea, though I walk through death's dark vale,
   yet will I fear none ill;
for thou art with me; and thy rod
   and staff me comfort still.

My table thou hast furnishèd
   in presence of my foes;
my head thou dost with oil anoint,
   and my cup overflows.

Goodness and mercy all my life
   shall surely follow me;
and in God's house for evermore
   my dwelling-place shall be.

Francis Rous (1579–1659)

There's a Friend for little children
Above the bright blue sky,
A Friend who never changes,
Whose love will never die;
Our earthly friends may fail us,
And change with changing years,
This Friend is always worthy
Of that dear name he bears.

There's a rest for little children
Above the bright blue sky,
Who love the blessèd Saviour,
And to the Father cry;
A rest from every trouble,
From sin and danger free,
Where every little pilgrim
Shall rest eternally.

There's a home for little children
Above the bright blue sky,
Where Jesus reigns in glory,
A home of peace and joy;
No home on earth is like it,
Nor can with it compare;
And every one is happy,
Nor could be happier, there.

A. Midlane

1   The Spirit lives to set us free,
     walk, walk in the light;
     He binds us all in unity,
     walk, walk in the light.
         Walk in the light,
         walk in the light,
         walk in the light,
         walk in the light of the Lord.

2 Jesus promised life to all,
  walk, walk in the light;
  the dead were wakened by His call,
  walk, walk in the light.
   Walk in the light . . .

3 He died in pain on Calvary,
  walk, walk in the light;
  to save the lost like you and me,
  walk, walk in the light.
   Walk in the light . . .

4 We know His death was not the end,
  walk, walk in the light;
  He gave His Spirit to be our friend,
  walk, walk, in the light.
   Walk in the light . . .

5 By Jesus' love our wounds are healed,
  walk, walk in the light;
  the Father's kindness is revealed,
  walk, walk in the light.
   Walk in the light . . .

6 The Spirit lives in you and me,
  walk, walk in the light;
  His light will shine for all to see,
  walk, walk in the light.
   Walk in the light . . .

Damian Lundy

1 Thine be the glory, risen, conquering Son,
  endless is the victory Thou o'er death hast won;
  angels in bright raiment rolled the stone away,
  kept the folded grave–clothes where Thy body lay.

> *Thine be the glory, risen, conquering Son,*
> *endless is the victory Thou o'er death hast won.*

2 Lo! Jesus meets us, risen from the tomb;
   lovingly He greets us, scatters fear and gloom;
   let the Church with gladness hymns of triumph sing,
   for her Lord now liveth; death hath lost its sting.
   Thine be the glory . . .

3 No more we doubt Thee, glorious Prince of life;
   life is nought without Thee: aid us in our strife;
   make us more than conquerors, through Thy deathless love:
   bring us safe through Jordan to Thy home above.
   Thine be the glory . . .

Edmund Budry (1854–1932),

tr. R. Birch Hoyle (1875–1939)

This day God gives me
strength of high heaven,
sun and moon shining,
flame in my hearth;
flashing of lightning,
wind in its swiftness,
deeps of the ocean,
firmness of earth.

This day God sends me
strength as my steersman,
might to uphold me,
wisdom as guide.
Your eyes are watchful,
Your ears are listening,
Your lips are speaking,
friend at my side.

God's way is my way,
God's shield is round me,
God's host defends me,
saving from ill;
angels of heaven,
drive from me always
all that would harm me,
stand by me still.

Rising, I thank you,
mighty and strong one,
king of creation,
giver of rest,
firmly confessing
threeness of Persons,
oneness of Godhead,
Trinity blest.

James Quinn (b. 1919), from eighth-century Irish

We're walking in the air
We're walking in the air,
We're floating in the moonlit sky,
The people far below
Are sleeping as we fly.

I'm holding very tight,
I'm riding in the midnight blue,
I'm finding I can fly
So high above with you.

All across the world
The villages go by like dreams,
The rivers and the hills
The forests and the streams.

Children gaze open-mouthed,
Taken by surprise,
Nobody down below
Believes their eyes.

We're surfing in the air,
We're swimming in the frozen sky,
We're drifting over icy mountains,
Floating by.

Suddenly, swooping low
On an ocean deep,
Rousing upward, mighty monster,
From his sleep.

We're floating in the air,
We're dancing in the moonlit sky,
And everyone who sees us
Greets us as we fly.

We're walking in the air.
We're walking in the air.

Sentences

Dear God, may we look backward with gratitude, forward with courage, upwards with confidence.

My bow I set in the cloud, sign of the covenant between myself and the earth.

Genesis, Chapter 9, verse 13, New English Bible

The eternal God is your dwelling place, and underneath are the everlasting arms.

Deuteronomy, Chapter 33, verse 27, Revised Standard Version of the Bible, Catholic Edition.

For all that has been – thanks; to all that will be – yes.

Dag Hammarskjöld

One crowded hour of glorious life is worth an age without a name.

Thomas Osbert Mordaunt

Grief is not forever – but love is.

Anonymous

Lord, I know you won't send any trouble today that you and I together cannot handle.

African Prayer

Then she is well, and nothing can be ill . . . And her immortal part with angels lives.

William Shakespeare

Death is not the extinguishing of the light, but the putting out of the lamp, because Dawn has come.

Rabindranath Tagore

He whom we love and lose is no longer where he was before; he is now wherever we are.

St John Chrysostom

Oh could I believe the living and dead inhabit one house
under the sky
and you my child run into your future for ever.

Frances Horovitz

Appendices and References

Appendix I

Further sources of help in bereavement

Some people may find it helpful to make contact with one of the organisations which offers support. This may be through telephone contact, group meetings or one to one support from someone who has previously experienced a similar bereavement. Some addresses and telephone numbers are given below.

Useful addresses
Alder Centre
For those affected by the death of a child
Royal Liverpool Children's Hospital
Alder Hey, Eaton Road, Liverpool L12 2AP
Child Death Helpline Freephone 0800 282986

British Humanist Association
47, Theobald's Road, London, WC1X 8SP
Helpline (24 hrs) 01608 652 063

Child Death Helpline
The Hospital for Sick Children
Great Ormond Street, London WC1N 3JH
Bereavement Services Co-ordinator 0171 813 8551
Child Death Helpline Freephone 0800 282986

Children in Focus, Specialist Funeral Service
David Chadwick
7 The Green, Woodburn Green
Bucks HP10 0EE
Tel: 01628 523253

Compassionate Friends
53, North Street, Bristol BS3 1EN
Helpline 0117 953 9639

Cot Death Society
4, Mansell Drive, Wash Common
Newbury, Berks. RG14 6TE
Tel: 01635 861771

Cruse – Bereavement Care
Cruse House, 126, Sheen Road, Richmond, Surrey TW9 1UR
Tel: 0181 940 4818
Helpline (Mon – Fri 9.30 – 5 p.m.) 0181 332 7227

Foundation for the Study of Infant Death
14, Halkin Street, London SW1X 7DP
Helpline (24 hrs) 0171 235 1721

Jewish Bereavement Counselling Service
1, Cyprus Gardens, London N3 1SP
Tel: 0181 387 4300 Ext.227

Parents of Murdered Children Support Group
(Linked to Compassionate Friends)
John and Irene Baldock,
15, Dean Road, Strood, Rochester, Kent ME2 3QH
Tel: 01634 718 299

REACT – Grants for equipment, holidays, funeral expenses, etc
St Luke's House, 270 Sandycombe Road
Kew, Surrey TW9 3NP
Tel: 0181 940 2575

Stillbirth and Neonatal Death Society
28, Portland Place, London W1N 4DE
Tel: 0171 436 7940
Helpline (24 hrs) 0171 436 5881

Support After Termination for Abnormality
73, Charlotte Street, London W1P 1LB
Tel: 0171 631 0280

Survival after Murder and Manslaughter
(Section of Victim Support)
Cranmer House, 39, Brixton Road, London SW9 6DZ
Tel: 0171 735 3838

Survivors of Suicide
Mary Lovegrove, 109, Abbeville Road, London SW4 9JL
Tel: 0171 622 7932
(Linked to Compassionate Friends)

Children's Hospices

Acorns
103, Oak Tree Lane, Selly Oak, Birmingham B29 6HZ
Tel: 0121 414 1741

Children's Hospice South West
Little Bridge House, Redlands Road, Fremington, Barnstaple EX31 2PZ
Tel: 01271 25270

Derian House
Chancery Road, Astley Village, Chorley, Lancashire PR7 1DH
Tel: 01257 233300

The Children's Hospice for the Eastern Region
Church Lane, Milton, Cambridge CB4 4AB
Tel: 01223 860 306

Francis House
390, Parrs Wood Road, Didsbury, Manchester M20 5NA
Tel: 0161 434 4118

Helen House
37, Leopold Street, Oxford OX4 1QT
Tel: 01865 728 251

Hope House
Nant Lane, Morda, Oswestry, Shropshire SY10 9BX
Tel: 01691 671 999

Martin House
Grove Road, Clifford, Wetherby, West Yorkshire LS23 6TX
Tel: 01937 845 045

Rachel House
Avenue Road, Kinross KY13 7EP
Tel: 01577 865777

Rainbows Children's Hospice
Lark Rise, Loughborough LE11 2HS
Tel: 01509 230 800

Quidenham Children's Hospice
Quidenham, Norfolk NR16 2PH
Tel: 01953 888 603.

Appendix II

Letters to Kim

The following two letters were written for Kim who died aged thirteen, after a bicycle accident. They were written by her classmates as their farewell to her, and the originals were placed in her coffin with her. Both are reproduced as they were written but the signatures have been removed so as to maintain the confidentiality of the children involved.

My dearest Kim,

I suppose you never thought I would be writing to you, as we always said everything to each other, that we needed to. No words can express how I, and many others, are feeling right now. I just wish I could have said goodbye, and given you a big hug. Miss Woodbridge was devestated but all the teachers have been brilliant. I don't think you ever realised how many people cared, liked, and even loved you.

The most difficult thing for me to picture is you, lying there with no heartbeat, mind you, I'm not surprised, you did so much with your life, your heart was probably absolutely pooped! Wow look! I've nearly written a whole page! This has got to be the longest letter I've ever written, and I haven't even finished yet! I will never, ever find such an ace best friend as you – I don't intend on looking because you'll always be there, no matter what. You're still there for a lot of people, we even keep a peg for you in P.E! It was the last one you used (we think) and we have a little piece of paper with your name written on it, and we put it on the peg. Mad aren't we! I hope you've read all the letters from everyone else, Fay has come up with this really wacky thing. Because it has been really sunny lately, she reckons that the sun is your bum! Crazy or what! Anyway, whenever the sun isn't shining, she always says 'Kim, show us your bum!!' You'll be glad to know that we drew 9 all, in the netball match against Park House. Lizzy organised it to have a minute's silence before the game. Oh yes, do you remember the photos I took of you when you came round? The ones with you on the exercise bike? Well I took them into school and everyone said that they wanted a copy so my mum got 40 copies. I could carry on writing for ever and ever, but eventually I'm sure I would bore you. There were a lot of things that you and I had already started planning for the future, for instance, you were going to be my matron of honour, remember? And I was going to be yours, we had it all sorted, or so we thought. The one thing in life most people are unprepared for is death, and boy oh boy, was I unprepared! It may sound silly, but you were not the type to die, mind you, who is?

I hope I haven't bored you too much, but if I keep going, I'll end up using a whole forest! Please do me the biggest favour possible and never leave me, always walk beside me.

All the love in the world,

From your best friend.

My dearest Kim,

I can't really put into words how I feel about what's happened. At one time I feel very angry and cross and at others just in great sorrow. I have cried about three or four times. I am sorry, I have tried more but I can't. I am not boasting here (I promise) but I would have died for you. You were so amazingly cool and perfect. You could have made Oxford or Cambridge and married and been the best interior decorator ever. I just dont understand why it had to be you. Oh, by the way, I am going to your funeral (hopefully) I hope you don't mind.

I know about you fancying me, Mandy and Gemma told me. I wish you had told me, I would have gone out with you because I knew that you were one of the nicest people I have ever known and I love you very much. I am not embarrased, and I hope you are not. The day I heard that you had had the accident I couldn't believe it.

Amy, Fay and myself had just got off the bus and we didn't see you and Mandy walking down. Then we saw Mandy and Del crying. I made a stupid joke about having some maths results. Fay said someone had died. Then we saw Simon crying and Ame asked him what was going on. He told us and Fay just burst into tears. Amy comforted her but when we got into the form room everyone was quiet and Kirsty was there. Then Amy just broke down. Mrs Baxter talked to them all through registration and I think it did a little good. I wanted to cry but I could only manage a small burst. Sorry! All day we were all crying. We all expected you to pull through. (We knew you would have brain damage and been paralysed from the neck down – I am glad for you that you didn't make it.) When we heard the news, Fay, Amy and Kirsty went into hysteria. I tried to comfort them but it did not do much good. Everyone was crying and the atmosphere was very, very bad.

When I got home I told my Mum. I immediately broke down so I am glad and I think it did some good. I told everyone I didn't so they would think I was hard. Stupid eh!

I couldn't accept that you had died and it was very hard to accept. I woke up the next morning and had got used to it though. Amy and Fay didn't get to it till the next morning.

I've told you how I felt about this thing and I still feel the same. I just didn't want you to die. Everyone in the year loves you really much. I never believed in God and in heaven until now and I'm still not sure about it. I just hope to God that you are OK and having a ball. I'm not sure whether I should believe or not. I would like to but it is unscientific and goes against my principals, but whatever happens, I'm not going to turn into the Pope or somethin' like that. When I grow up I am going to be a nuerologist so I can help people to live because now I know how ****ing bad it all is. I wish this had never happened but unfortunately it has and we've got to make the best of it. Kim, I will always and forever love you so,

    With all my heart,
    love (times infinite)
    from your 4th best friend.
    I LOVE YOU.

Appendix III

Reflections on death in childhood (Originally published in 1987)

During the past four years I have been involved in varying degrees in the death of about 70 people, most of them children and teenagers. Almost anything worth while that I have learnt about death, I have learnt from those young people and from those closest to them. Perhaps the most important thing has been the gradual recognition that however ill at ease and maladroit Western society is in the face of death, given permission and a loving, affirming environment, the individual will meet death with what I can describe only as a severe beauty.

Death is familiar to us in war, in holocaust, and in massive famine disasters, but we know it as remote control statistics. Death is no longer the familiar part of the domestic neighbourhood scene that it was 100 or even 50 years ago. Improved living conditions, health care, and highly developed skills in medicine and surgery, the breakdown of the extended family and the close knit local community, the tendency for the fatally ill, even the elderly, to be taken away to hospital or institution, all contribute to an unfamiliarity with death. Many people will reach middle age without ever having been in the presence of death and possibly without having attended a funeral.

The more sophisticated our society becomes and the more it pays homage to intellect and powers of reasoning the more ill at ease it is with death and that which lies beyond. Religion, belief in that which cannot be proved, and the readiness to allow ourselves to be led beyond our ken into the realms of mystery are things less and less to be trusted. Sometimes those who wield the greatest power and possess the greatest wealth are those who fare worst for here, finally, is something which neither money nor position can win back − life itself.

'Sparing' feelings
Our society does not handle death well. How often are the relatives asked to leave the hospital bedside when the patient takes a turn for the worse and the end seems perilously near and are only called back when it is all over? Perhaps it is because 'heroic' measures are to be taken to forestall the end and the intention is to spare the relatives unnecessary distress, but it may be

worth considering whether some relatives would rather be there even so; I do wonder who it is who is afraid and whose feelings we are trying to protect.

When it is all over we often seem to feel that now the best way to spare the feelings of the bereaved is to act with great haste. The funeral director is called in to remove the body as quickly as possible; the relatives are seen walking away down the hospital drive with a plastic bag or a suitcase containing the dead person's effects within an hour or so of death. The doctor is asked to prescribe sedatives or hypnotics, and the funeral is planned on the first available day. The service itself is kept short and to the point and emotions are suppressed. Everyone is afraid of emotional behaviour, people stand at the ready in case the bereaved should lose all control and throw themselves into the grave after the coffin or tear apart the closed curtains in the crematorium. It is with a sense of relief that people repair to tea and sandwiches and the comfortable exchange of harmless small talk.

Some relatives and friends will be responsive to the need that the bereaved have of support and friendship over the next weeks but after that they will be few and far between. Then the general attitude prevails: best get back to normal and avoid all circumstances or conversations which serve as reminders of the one who has died. It is at this point that grief, which is a *natural response to loss*, is at risk of becoming suppressed and distorted to the extent that the natural response becomes a psychiatric disorder. I believe that the reason why so many bereaved people end up needing professional counselling or psychiatric treatment is that the rest of us are afraid. Face to face with grief we feel inadequate or embarrassed, we make ourselves scarce and fervently hope that there is an 'expert' around to handle the situation. I hasten to add that this is not intended as a condemnation of the work of bereavement counsellors or psychiatrists. I readily accept that there may be factors in the life of the bereaved, quite apart from the reactions of others, which can benefit from professional expertise. Rather, I condemn a society which prefers to have such things dealt with at a safe distance, clinically and antiseptically, and seems to absolve itself from the responsibility for making itself available to be alongside and to stay alongside and to take on board some of the suffering and grief of others.

Trusting instinct
One beautiful autumn day a 10-month-old baby boy died. We knew that he could not live very long but his actual death came on a day when he seemed particularly alert and happy. When he died his mother carried him into the garden, walked and sat with him in her arms for a couple of hours, often with one of us beside her, occasionally alone with him. She cried gently and talked to him. She remembered the day that he was born, also a beautiful sunny day; she talked of all the joy that he had brought into life and of the pain. Then, in her own time, she carried him back into their

room and lay down with him still in her arms and slept for an hour. Then, and only then, was she ready to wash and dress him with very great love and care and without any sense of hurry. She chose the clothes he was to wear and the toys he was to have with him. She had already seen the small room, furnished much like a bedroom but able to be kept very cold, where he was to lie for the next few days. She carried him there. The little boy's mother and father visited him often in that small room, sometimes brushing his hair or rearranging his toys, sometimes lifting him out of his cot and sitting with him, uncurling his fingers and looking again at his hands, kissing him in the nape of his neck, lost in grief and in the wonder of the miracle that was their son. All they needed was our permission, spoken or unspoken, to do it their way, the way they knew instinctively, and our presence in the background and the knowledge that we felt pain and wonder too and were not afraid to show it.

As we cope with life so will we cope with death. Difficulties and conflict in relationships in the ordinary course of events may not disappear in the presence of death, indeed in the midst of distress they may be painfully exaggerated. It is not for those of us who are involved professionally to take sides but rather to believe the best of each individual and to try to support without discrimination. One relative may remain dry eyed and controlled throughout; the other hysterical and seemingly out of control. We have to accept both and not be thrown off balance by either. To whom is the hysterical reaction of a newly bereaved teenager a threat? In the privacy of a room can that young person not be allowed to lie down beside the dead brother or sister or hold the child or scream to God to bring this person he or she loves back to life again? And if that teenager asks to be left alone with the dead child for a time can we not take the risk? All this may be an essential part in the whole process of healing. Each member of the family, not just the chief mourner, has a right and a need to grieve and to express that grief in his or her own way.

Reality is gentler than fantasy

Children's fantasy and imagination are highly developed. I believe that the reality of seeing a dead brother or sister is easier to cope with and kinder to the child's sensitivities than the ordeal of experience by fantasy. On seeing her dead sister and showing no emotion and making no comment, it was several hours before a 6-year-old said, 'I thought when you were dead there was only your head. I thought all your skin peeled off.' And then still later, 'Where is she? How can she be in heaven when she's still in that little room?' I have found that the analogy of a shell or a chrysalis or a house can be useful. The important part, the living part, has gone on and this is all that is left behind. An exceptional 11-year-old spoke of his body as a reflection. 'It is how you recognise me for who I am. When I die I will leave my reflection behind but the real me won't die; when I die, the real me will go to that very special place.' Many children have experienced the death of a pet. 'When my dog died he left his skin behind,' was the comment of a 7-year-old. A 4-year-old girl was trying to come to terms with the death of her 3-year-old cousin. Helping her mother to clear the coal fire at home she said, 'He's gone like the coal. Just the ashes left behind.'

We must guard against using the adjective 'peaceful' indiscriminately when describing death or the face of the child after death. If it is untrue it may distance us from the family who sense that this is one of the games that people play. It is true, however, that an hour or two after death relatives will often be comforted by the fact that the dead child does indeed look peaceful and even seems to smile. They may spend time with the child, greatly comforted, despite their grief, that 'he looks so like himself'. Then almost imperceptibly after two or three days a change comes about and the relatives will remark on how it's 'not him any more', or on how 'he's gone'. Here nature itself takes its share in bringing about acceptance of what has happened and in carrying those who grieve a stage further on.

I hesitate to write about religion as a separate issue. Two things are clear to me. One is that mystery and a sense of awe surround death and whatever lies beyond it. The second is that an effect of love and grief exposed, the soul laid bare, is to bring forth reverence in the beholder. Here we find ourselves beyond the realms of reason crossing all barriers of different faiths. I would say that we share the experience of treading on holy ground. However much they may have ignored or scorned any kind of formal religion in the past, I do not think that there are many parents who do not wonder about the existence of a God when their child is dying. I have yet to meet a mother or father who has believed, at the moment of death, that their child ceased to exist. 'She was so special and I loved her so much that there has to be a God to love her and a heaven where she can dance and play and be happy,' said one young mother. Many parents will want someone to pray with them when their child is dying or after death. Speaking as a Christian, I know that there are many times when I can say only, 'I do not know' in response to questions about the meaning of it all. Yet for myself I hold fast to the conviction that death is a beginning rather than an end.

One young mother who had experienced most kinds of deprivation and degradation in her own short life was resolved that her little daughter was going to have the life and the love that she herself had not known. The news that the baby girl had a rare, life-threatening disease only strengthened that resolve and she cared for the child through the months of illness with singleminded devotion. Finally, she held her child through the last hours of life and we talked. The little girl breathed more and more slowly and then took one final breath. The mother looked up and said, 'Is that it?' I nodded. 'It's incredible,' she said. 'It's like giving birth again. After all the waiting and the pain, she's born. I've done it. She's there.' This was the spontaneous reaction of someone with little education and no formal religion. After two or three minutes she handed me the child saying, 'Is there some wine in the house? Everyone must drink to her. We must celebrate.' Her grief in the following months has been as profound and as harrowing as anyone can experience but that does not in any way deny the rightness of her immediate, instinctive response at the moment of death. She dressed her daughter in a red velvet dress that she had made for the occasion, painted her minute finger nails, and bedecked her with tiny jewels.

The days following death

The choice of clothes is intensely personal. For some it will be a traditional white shroud, for others a jogging suit or jeans, for yet others the clothes worn for First Communion or for parties. One little girl wore a ballet dress and new pink ballet shoes; a boy was dressed in his treasured Batman outfit. What matters is that it is right for this particular child and family and it can happen only if we provide an assumed permission to do it their way. I have a haunting memory of the distress a mother experienced when she was taken to see her child after he had died unexpectedly under anaesthetic. He was in a white shroud with his hair neatly brushed forward. She hardly recognised him. She longed for him to be in his jeans and sweat shirt with his hair rumpled back as it had always been. In all her grief she was grateful to the person who had taken such care to make him look nice, but he wasn't any longer her son.

Here I should add that although I write from the context of a children's hospice, many of 'our' children die, quite rightly, in their own homes. Most of what I write is, I believe, equally possible and helpful there. I have been privileged to be with several families when their child died at home and the child has remained in his or her own bedroom until the day of the funeral. Nothing has been hurried, everything has been spontaneous and natural.

Some parents will want to register the death of their child themselves, others will be grateful to be relieved of the responsibility. For many the decision between burial and cremation is a painful one. Either alternative may seem intolerable to contemplate – the gradual decomposition of the body beneath the ground or the rapid consuming of the body by the flames. The thought of the child's hair and face being burnt is especially distressing for many parents. One mother asked to tour the crematorium before deciding. The director of the crematorium could not have been more helpful, showing us behind the scenes and explaining the whole process, answering all questions honestly and straightforwardly. Children who know that they are going to die will often express an opinion. One boy who had a progressively handicapping disease wanted his body cremated because, he said, it hadn't been much use to him in life. Another child wanted to be buried because she knew that her parents would want to visit her grave. For some of course religion will be the deciding factor.

Parents will often want to choose their child's coffin, and they must not be hurried in their choice or indeed in making any of the arrangements for their child. Toys or special treasures may be put in the coffin, though there will be others who take the view that such things are trivial and inappropriate. Letters or cards written to the child after death and placed in the coffin may be another step towards healing and wholeness for the one who writes. The planning of the funeral service is a personal thing and the parents' need is for someone who will give gentle guidance and perhaps the suggestion of some sort of framework allowing plenty of opportunity for the choice of music and words appropriate to their child. Just as the clothes the child wears are a matter of personal choice, so are the clothes worn by the bereaved at the funeral. We may be horrified at a young couple, whom we know to be very hard up financially, going out to buy new black outfits for their child's funeral. But for them this may be an integral part of their own instinctive ritual of grieving.

Many people say how much they dread the day of the funeral itself. In the event most will say that they found it a much more helpful experience than they had dared to hope. 'Is it awful to say I enjoyed it?' asked one mother. 'I didn't know how many people loved him and cared.' Attendance at the funeral comes to be seen as a tribute. It is also a token of love and support to the parents and the family.

Forewarned is forearmed

I think it is helpful to warn parents or other newly bereaved people that other people's pious platitudes can be insensitive and hurtful; that however close the relationship between two people may be, they may grieve differently; and that the healing of grief is a very long, slow process. It is never complete; parents will never 'get over' the death of their child.

The pious platitudes are seemingly endless. 'Oh well, his sufferings are over now.' 'Poor little thing, it's a mercy really.' 'She is at peace.' 'Time will heal.' And worse follows: 'You're young enough to have another.' 'It's a good thing you've got the baby – that'll take your mind off it.' If there is someone to laugh with about these remarks it helps, and so too does the recognition that people want to be helpful and they do mean well. It's just that most people do feel inadequate and uncomfortable in the face of death and, if forced to say something, all sorts of things trip off the tongue.

Individuals grieve differently. For parents whose child has died there is the added complication that they are probably both worn down physically and emotionally, drained of the psychological resources they once had for meeting each other half way. One may grieve openly, the other finding it difficult to express grief. For both there will be an appalling vacuum at the centre of their lives, a sense of their arms being left empty. Half waking in the morning the reflex reaction may be to go and tend the sick child and then the nightmare of the realisation that there is no child to tend. A whole empty day stretches ahead and the one left at home may envy the one who goes out to work, or sometimes vice versa. It can be painful putting on a cheerful face at work. However sympathetic colleagues or work mates may be initially, the continuing grief becomes uncomfortable for them. Taking the surviving child to playgroup or school other parents tend to scatter as in the presence of one with a contagious disease. Sometimes the bereaved parent who takes most care with appearance or make up in a desperate attempt to 'put a face on it' and keep going is the one who gets least sympathy and support because he or she seems to be coping.

Parents and siblings may manifest grief in different ways. The overt grief, the crying, the sorrow, the reminiscing is easier to take than the pettiness, the short temper, the clinging behaviour of the children, the rows seemingly over nothing. It needs someone to say, 'It's all right. All these things are a very natural part of your grief. You haven't become a hateful person, neither has your husband, your wife, your child, your parent. Your anger against the doctor, the hospital, yourself, or God, is natural and safe. Give it time. Hang on somehow. A day will come when you will wake up and think, "Yes, there is some point in being alive".' And it needs a friend or friends who will listen, however endlessly repetitious the conversation, who knows when to hug and when to stand back, who won't be offended by hurtful remarks, but will be alongside and readily available. Yet in all that I say about this and about all reactions and responses to death and bereavement there are exceptions. We each have to be sensitive and to recognise that we may not be the right person and may not be acceptable alongside, and that for some people grief is a private thing and must be respected as such.

For some a self-help group such as Compassionate Friends or a support group such as Cruse may be useful. Those who have themselves experienced a similar type of bereavement can help as no one else can; the rest of us should guard against saying, 'I know how you feel' – we don't.

Possessions and memories

Sorting out clothes, toys, and other possessions is very personal. Some people will feel instinctively that this should be done quickly. I think I would warn against a too ruthless clearing out. In the long term some of the child's personal things may be comforting rather than the reverse. For others the pain of sorting through possessions may be too painful to be tackled for many months. I think that they should be reassured that this is all right and that there is no hurry. There are extremes of course which might be judged as unhealthy – photographs quickly destroyed or put away and all evidence of the child removed, or the bedroom preserved untouched as a sanctuary through many years. But on the whole, given permission and reassurance, the family will know instinctively what is best for them. In conversation a caring and thoughtful man expressed great concern for a neighbour of his. Some weeks previously the neighbour's son had run across the road and been killed. Since the funeral the child's mother had taken to going to church each Sunday morning. Her husband took her to church by car and then walked through some woods by a river where he and his boy had often gone fishing. The man who was speaking to me was sure that this was unhealthy and needed to be discouraged. I hope I persuaded him that it was probably the healthiest thing that his friend could do – in the sense of health meaning making whole.

Favourite places, anniversaries, seasons with their associated flowers and smells, all these may be poignant reminders and need to be acknowledged. They are poignant not only for the parents – they may be just as painful for the surviving brother or sister. Other things hurt the surviving children too: the nagging feeling that the one who died was everyone's favourite and that they would have preferred it if you had died; the guilt of remembered remarks from the past like, 'I wish you were dead', 'I'll kill you', 'Drop dead'; the fear that you might die too; the innocent question, 'How many brothers and sisters have you?' And surrounding all this, parents who burst into tears unexpectedly or lose their temper unreasonably.

It does all take a very long time. More than one parent has said that they were grateful that we had given them early warning of this. Without such a warning they would have felt they were going out of their minds or abnormal – different from other people – when there seemed to be no light at the end of the tunnel well into the second year of bereavement. I have always been grateful to the father who told me that the second year was for him worse, if anything, than the first and that by the beginning of the third year he was just beginning to feel there was some point in living. I believe that the pain of bereavement is greatly intensified when society expects you to get over it quickly and you are left feeling stranded because you are a long way from complete recovery. After a gathering of bereaved families a mother who lost her baby daughter, her father, and her year-old son within four years of each other wrote, 'If we go to any function people ask how many children we have; we have now learnt to say three. On Sunday it was so lovely to be able to say five. After all they were parts of our love and lives and with you they stay with us, outside they have to be locked away.'

Conclusion

Saying to parents whose child has died, 'You will get over it,' is like saying, 'One day it will seem as if he never existed.' Nothing could be more hurtful. They don't want him written out of existence. But given time, given permission to be who they are, given reassurance to behave instinctively, given love and friendship, I believe that they will have the best chance to adjust to what has happened and grow towards healing and wholeness. Despite society's fear of death and ineptitude in the face of death, I believe that every individual has the potential within to meet death with a severe beauty which in no way denies grief. Being alongside such families you absorb some of their grief. But you also share some of the good things – learning to think of time in terms of depth rather than length; enjoying the swift growth of real friendship; bypassing the usual obstacles of class, creed, colour, age, education; having 'all one's sensitivities heightened' as one father put it. And you begin to recognise and reverence the nobility and beauty in every man, woman, and child because tragedy lifts the mask of pretence and truth is revealed.

I thank Professor J. D. Baum for his help in preparing this article.

Reproduced by permission of the BMJ Publishing Group.

Example of a Service Sheet

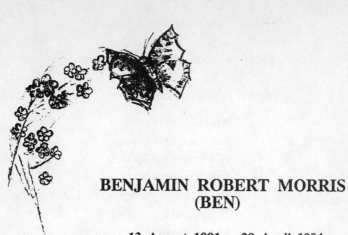

BENJAMIN ROBERT MORRIS
(BEN)

13 August 1991 – 29 April 1994

Their precious charge so meek and mild
Is heaven's very special child.

No more pain, no more tears
Just wonderful memories
That will last for years.

4 May 1994
All Saints Chapel
Oxford

Music   'Ben' by the Jackson 5

Welcome and Opening Prayer

Hymn Morning has broken

Morning has broken
Like the first morning,
Blackbird has spoken
Like the first bird.
Praise for the singing!
Praise for the morning,
Praise for them springing
Fresh from the Word.

Sweet the rain's new fall,
Sunlit from heaven,
Like the first dewfall
On the first grass.
Praise for the sweetness
Of the wet garden,
Sprung in completeness
Where His feet pass.

Mine is the sunlight!
Mine is the morning
Born of the one light
Eden saw play!
Praise with elation,
Praise every morning,
God's·re-creation
Of the new day.

Eleanor Farjeon

Poem A Child Loaned

'I'll lend you for a little time a child of mine,' he said,
'For you to love the while he lives, and mourn for when he's dead.
He may be six or seven years, or even two or three,
But will you till I call him back, take care of him for me?
He'll bring his charm to gladden you, and, should his stay be brief,
You'll have his lovely memories as solace for your grief.

I cannot promise he will stay, since all from earth return,
But there are lessons taught down there I want this child to learn.
I've looked the wide world over in my search for teachers true And
from the throng that crowd life's lanes I have selected you.
Now will you give him all your love, nor think the labour's vain,
Nor hate me when I come to call and take him back again?'

I fancied that I heard them say, 'Dear Lord, thy will be done,
For all the joys thy child shall bring the risk of grief we'll run.
We'll shelter him with tenderness, we'll love him while we may
And for the happiness we've known, for ever grateful stay.
But, should the angels call for him much sooner than we planned
We'll brave the bitter grief that comes and try to understand.'

Author unknown

Reading Mark 10, verses 14–17

He said to them, 'Let the children come to me; do not try to stop them; for the kingdom of God belongs to such as these. I tell you, whoever does not accept the kingdom of God like a child will never enter it.' And he put his arms round them, laid his hands upon them and blessed them.

New English Bible

Homily Michael Smith, Chaplain of Helen House

Hymn   All Things Bright and Beautiful

Chorus   All things bright and beautiful,
all creatures great and small,
all things wise and wonderful,
the Lord God made them all.

Each little flower that opens,
each little bird that sings,
He made their glowing colours,
He made their tiny wings.

The cold wind in the winter,
the pleasant summer sun,
the ripe fruits in the garden,
He made them every one.

He gave us eyes to see them,
and lips that we might tell
how great is God Almighty,
who has made all things well.

Mrs C. F. Alexander (1818–1895)

Prayers

Poem   Welcoming a Special Child

A meeting was held quite far from earth;
It's time again for another birth.
Said the angels to the Lord above,
'This special child will need much love.

He may not run or laugh or play;
His thoughts may seem quite far away.
In many ways he won't adapt,
And he'll be known as handicapped.

So let's be careful where he's sent;
We want his life to be content.
Please Lord, find parents who
Will do a special job for you.

They will not realise straight away
The leading role they're asked to play;
But with this child sent from above
Comes stronger faith and richer love.

And soon they'll know the privilege given
In caring for their child from heaven;
Their precious charge, so meek and mild,
Is heaven's very special child.'

Edna Massimilla

Poems chosen by Jacki

For Ben

Eyes that twinkle sunshine,
A face that breaks your heart,
That special look of innocence
Remains while we're apart.
We had you for a short while,
But you brought so many joys,
Now play in peace our baby,
Enjoy your angel toys.
Time will bring us comfort
While waiting for the day
When we will be together again
Not just a whisper away.

There was a Child once

He came to play in my garden
He was quite pale and silent
Only when he smiled I knew all about him
I knew all his thoughts
And I knew the feel of his hands
and the most intimate tones of his voice
I led him down each secret path
Showing him the hiding place of all the treasures
I let him play with them, every one
I put my singing thoughts in a little silver cage
and gave them to him to keep
It was very dark in the garden
but never dark enough for us.
On tiptoe we walked amongst the deepest shades
We bathed in the shadow pools beneath the trees
Pretending we were under the sea.
Once – near the boundary of the garden
We heard steps passing along the world road
Oh, how frightened we were!
I whispered, have you ever walked along that road?
He nodded and we shook the tears from our eyes.
There was a child once
He came, quite alone to play in my garden
He was pale and silent
When we met we kissed each other
But when he went away, we did not even wave.

Commendation and Committal

Everyone is invited to Helen House while the family
goes to the Crematorium. Thanks for all the love and
care we had from everyone at Helen House.

Thanks for choosing us, Ben.

Music   Tears in Heaven by Eric Clapton

Further reading

Baum, J. D., Dominica, F., Woodward, R. N. (1990) *Listen. My Child Has a Lot of Living to Do*. Oxford University Press, Oxford.

Bentley, J., Best, A., Hunt, J. (1994) *Funerals: A Guide*. Hodder and Stoughton, London.

Cooper, A., Harpin, V. (1991) 'This is our Child'. Oxford University Press.

Dyregrov, A. (1994) *Grief in Children – a handbook for adults*. Jessica Kingsley Publications.

Harris, P. (1995) *What to Do When Someone Dies*. Which? Consumer Guides.

Hill, L. (1994) *Caring for Dying Children and Their Families*. Chapman and Hall, London.

Neuberger, J. (1987) *Caring for Dying People of Different Faiths*. Austen Cornish and Lisa Sainsbury Foundation, London.

Secretan, T. (1995) *Going into Darkness: Fantastic Coffins from Africa*. Thames and Hudson.

Walter, T. (1990) *Funerals and How to Improve Them*. Hodder and Stoughton, London.

Wilkinson, T. (1991) *The Death of a Child*. Julia Macrae Books, London.

Worswick, J. (1993) *A House Called Helen*, HarperCollins, London.

Living With Sorrow, a Helen House publication. Obtainable from Helen House, 37 Leopold Street, Oxford OX4 1QT.

Index of Sources and Acknowledgements

Prayers

Adam, David, *Prayer for a Loved One Departed* © 1992 by David Adam. Published by Tim Tiley Ltd, Bristol. **57**

Anonymous. Source unknown. **50, 52**

Anonymous, *Act of Farewell*. Used by kind permission of SANDS (Stillbirth and Neonatal Death Society) **58**

Anonymous, Gaelic prayer. **58**

Anonymous, Gaelic rune. **58**

Anonymous, Sarum prayer. **47**

Bible: *Revised Standard Version of the Bible, Catholic Edition*, © copyright 1966 by the Division of Christian Education of the National Council of the Churches of Christ in the USA. Used with permission. **58**

Common Prayer, Book of, the rights in which are vested in the Crown. This extract reproduced by permission of the Crown's Patentee, Cambridge University Press. **55**

Donne, John, from *XXVI Sermons* (1660), 29 February, 1627/8. **45**

Eimer, Robert, OMI and O'Malley, Sarah, OSB. *The Blessing of the Body* was reprinted with permission from *In the Potter's Hands: Nine Wake Services* by Robert Eimer OMI and Sarah O'Malley OSB, © 1988 by Resource Publications, Inc. 160E Virginia Street #290, San Jose, CA 95112. All Rights Reserved. **57**

Francis of Assisi, St. (attributed). **52**

Funeral Service for a Child Dying Near the Time of Birth. Material is copyright © The Central Board of Finance of The Church of England and is reproduced with permission. **45, 50, 53**

Jewish Funeral Service Prayer Book. Forms of Prayer for Jewish Worship, Funeral Service, Reform Synagogues of Great Britain, London, 1974. Used with permission. **53, 54, 55, 56**

Newman, John Henry, From 'Wisdom and Innocence' in *Sermons Bearing on Subjects of the Day* (1843), no. 20. **49, 55**

New Zealand Prayer Book. This copyright material is taken from *A New Zealand Prayer Book, He Karakia Mihinare o Aotearoa*, and is used with permission. **46, 47, 48, 52, 55**

Penn, William. **56**

Prayer Book as Proposed in 1928. Material is copyright © The Central Board of Finance of The Church of England and is reproduced with permission. **45, 54**

Reform Judaism Prayer Book. Forms of Prayer for Jewish Worship, Funeral Service, Reform Synagogues of Great Britain, London, 1974. Used with permission. **51**

Revised Funeral Rites, General Synod of the Scottish Episcopal Church. Printed by permission. **46, 47, 48, 49**

Smith, Michael D. Reproduced by kind permission of the author. **49, 51**

Webb, Pauline. Used by kind permission of the author. **45, 53**

Scriptural Readings

New English Bible, © Oxford University Press and Cambridge University Press 1961, 1970. Used with permission. **61, 62, 63, 64, 66, 159**

New Jerusalem Bible, published and copyright 1985 by Darton, Longman and Todd Ltd and Doubleday and Co. Inc., and used by permission of the publishers. **61, 62, 64, 66**

Revised Standard Version of the Bible, Catholic Edition, copyright 1966 by the Division of Christian Education of the National Council of the Churches of Christ in the USA. Used with permission. **59, 60, 63, 64, 67**

Non-Scriptural Readings

Anonymous, source unknown. **96, 98, 99, 100, 101, 102, 103, 104, 105, 159**

Bach, Richard, from *Jonathan Livingstone Seagull*. **68**

Blake, William, from 'Auguries of innocence'. **69**

Bonhoeffer, Dietrich, *Letters and Papers from Prison*, SCM Press 1953. **69**

Brooke, Rupert, source unknown. **70**

Byron, George Gordon, Lord, (adapted), source unknown. **71**

Frankl, Victor, *Man's Search for Meaning*. Reproduced by permission of Hodder and Stoughton Ltd. **72**

Fynn, *Mister God, This is Anna*, HarperCollins Publishers Ltd. **72**

Gibran, Kahlil, from *The Prophet* (1923). **73, 74, 75**

Giranjali, Poems of Gitanjali, Element Books 1982. Reproduced by kind permission of Mrs Kushi Badruddin. **75, 77**

Grenfell, Joyce, from *Joyce by Herself and Her friends* published by Futura. © The Joyce Grenfell Memorial Trust 1980 and reproduced with permission. **77**

Grollman Earl. Reproduced by kind permission of the author. **78**

Haskyns, Minnie Louise, from 'God knows', *Desert* (1908). **78**

Hathaway, Mary, from *Hope for when I'm hurting* © Mary Hathaway with Permission. Published by Lion plc. **78**

Hemmy, Lindy, source unknown. **79**

Holland, Henry Scott, from 'The King of Terrors', sermon preached on Whitsunday, 1910, in *Facts of the Faith* (1919). **79**

Hugo, Victor, from *Toilers of the Sea* (1866). **80**

Jarrett, Bede, OP, from *No Abiding City* © The Dominican Order and used by kind persmission of the Prior Provincial. **80**

Jonson, Ben, from 'To the immortal Memory and Friendship of that Noble Pair, Sir Lucius Cary and Sir Henry Morison' (1640). **81**

Keller, Helen, source unknown. **81**

Lewis, C. S., from *The Last Battle*. Reproduced by permission of Harper Collins Publishers Ltd. **81**

Littleboy, William, source unknown. **82**

Massimilla, Edna, source unknown. **82, 160**

McKenzie, Anna, ©. Used by permission of the author. **83**

Milne, A.A., from *The House at Pooh Corner*. Reproduced by permission of Reed Books. **85**

Penn, William, from *Some Fruits of Solitude* (1693). **85**

Pizer, Marjorie, from *To You the Living*. Reproduced by kind permission of Harper Collins Publishers (Australia). **86**

Price Hughes, A., source unknown. **86**

Shawe, Marilyn (ed.), from *Enduring, Sharing, Loving*. Published and copyright © 1992 Darton, Longman and Todd Ltd in association with The Alder Centre and used by the permission of the publishers. **86**

Stickney, Doris, *Water bugs and dragonflies*. Reproduced by permission of Cassell plc. **87**

Tagore, Rabindranath, *I Was Not Aware of the Moment*. Reproduced by kind permission of Macmillan General Books. **89**

Taylor, Bishop John V., from *Weep Not For Me*, © 1985 WCC Publications, World Council of Churches, Geneva, Switzerland. Reproduced by kind permission. **89**

Thomas, R. S., from *Later Poems*. Reproduced by kind permission of Papermac. **90**

Tolkien, J. R. R., from *The Hobbit*. Reproduced by kind permission of George Allen and Unwin, an imprint of HarperCollins Publishers Ltd. **90**

Traherne, Thomas, *Centuries of Meditations* (discovered 1896–7 and first published 1908). **91**

Travers, P. L., from *Mary Poppins*. Reproduced by permission of HarperCollins Publishers Ltd. **92**

Vanstone, W. H., from *Love's Endeavour, Love's Expense*. Published by and copyright © 1977 Darton, Longman and Todd Ltd and used by permission of the publishers. **92**

Vogel, Lindon Jane, from *Helping a Child Understand Death*. **94**

Wordsworth, William, 'Ode: Intimations of Immortality' (1807). **94**

Young, Graeme C., from *Children, Death and Bereavement* by Pat Wynnejones, reproduced with kind permission. **94**

Hymns and songs

Alexander, C. F., 'All things bright and beautiful'. **107, 160**

Anonymous, 'Caribbean Lord's Prayer' © McCrimmon Publishing Company Ltd. Used by permission. **128**

Anonymous, 'Give me oil in my lamp'. **114**

Anonymous, 'Kum Ba Yah'. **119**

Bible Society, 'Do not be worried and upset', from *Sing Good News* © 1980. Used with permission. **112**

Blake, Howard, 'Walking in the Air' From *The Snowman*. Copyright © 1982, 1994 Highbridge Music Ltd. Reproduced by kind permission Faber Music Ltd, on behalf of Highbridge Music Ltd. **133**

Bridges, Robert, 'All my hope on God is founded', after Joachim Neander, from the *Yattendon Hymnal* by permission of Oxford University Press. **106**

Budry, Edmund, 'Thine be the glory risen, conquering Son'. **131**

Byrne, Mary Elizabeth (tr.), 'Be thou my vision, O Lord of my heart', from the *Book of Gael*, selected and edited by Eleanor Hull. Used by kind permission of the Estate of the translator and versifier and Chatto and Windus, publishers. **109**

Carter, Sydney, 'I danced in the morning', © 1963. Reproduced by permission of Stainer and Bell Ltd, London, England. **115**

Crossman, Samuel, 'My song is love unknown' (1664). **125**

Crum, J. M. C., 'Now the green blade riseth from the buried grain', from *The Oxford Book of Carols* (1928). Reproduced by permission of Oxford University Press. **127**

Dearmer, Percy, (1867–1936), 'He who would valiant be' (after John Bunyan), from *The English Hymnal*, by permission of Oxford University Press. **115**

Evans, David J., 'Be still for the presence of the Lord, the Holy One is here'. Copyright © 1986 Kingsway's Thankyou Music, PO Box 75, Eastbourne, East Sussex, BN23 6NW, UK. Used by permission. **108**

Farjeon, Eleanor, 'Morning has broken', from *The Children's Bells* (OUP), by permission of David Higham Associates. **124, 158**

Francis, Prayer of St, 'Make me a channel of your peace', Dedicated to Mrs Frances Tracy, © 1967, OCP Publications, 5536 NE Hassalo, Portland, OR 97213. All rights reserved. Used with permission. **122**

Gellert, Christian F., 'Jesus Lives! Thy terrors now'. **118**

Gillman, Bob, 'Bind us together Lord'. Copyright © 1977 Kingsway's Thankyou Music, PO Box 75, Eastbourne, East Sussex, BN23 6NW, UK. Used by permission. **110**

Howard, Brian, 'If I were a butterfly'. Copyright © 1974 Mission Hills Music/Kingsway's Thankyou Music, PO Box 75, Eastbourne, E. Sussex, BN23 6NT, UK. Used by kind permission of Kingsway's Thankyou Music. **117**

Kendrick, Graham, 'Lord, the light of your love is shining'. Copyright © 1987 Make Way Music, PO Box 263, Croydon, Surrey CR9 5AP, UK.

Lundy, Damian, 'The Spirit lives to set us free'. Copyright © Kevin Mayhew Ltd. Reproduced by permission from *Hymns Old and New,* Licence No 698092. **130**

Mathams, Walter J., 'Jesus friend of little children'. Reproduced by permission of Oxford University Press. **118**

McClellan, Sue, Paculabo, John and Rycroft, Keith, 'Colours of day'. Copyright © 1974 Kingsway's Thank You Music, PO Box 75, Eastbourne, East Sussex, BN23 6NW, UK. Used by permission. **110**

A. Midlane, 'There's a Friend for little children'. **130**

Newton, John, 'Amazing grace', *Olney Hymns* (1779). **108**

Quinn, James, 'This day God given me', from *Praise for All Seasons*. Permission granted by Geoffrey Chapman, an imprint of Cassell plc. **132**

Rinkart, Martin, 'Now thank we all our God'. **126**

Rous, Francis, 'The Lord's my Shepherd, I'll not want', *The Scottish Psalter* (1650). **129**

SANDS, 'Fleetingly known, yet ever remembered'. Used by kind permission of SANDS (Stillbirth and Neonatal Death Society). May be sung to the tune 'Morning has broken'. **113**

Sarum, Horae BVM, 'God be in my head and in my understanding'. **114**

Struther, Jan, 'Lord of all hopefulness, Lord of all joy', from *Enlarged Songs of Praise*, by permission of Oxford University Press. **120**

Vanstone, W. H., 'A hymn to the Creator', reproduced by kind permission of J. W. Shore. **123**

Wesley, Charles, 'Love Divine all loves excelling'. **121**

Whittier, John Greenleaf, 'Dear Lord and Father of mankind'. **111**

Sentences

Anonymous, source unknown. **135**

Anonymous, African prayer. **136**

Bible: *New English Bible,* © Oxford University Press and Cambridge University Press 1961, 1970. Used with permission. **135**

Bible: *Revised Standard Version of the Bible, Catholic Edition*, copyright © 1966 by the Division of Christian Education of the National Council of the Churches of Christ in the USA. Used with permission. **135**

Chrysostom, St John. **136**

Hammarskjöld, Dag. Reproduced by kind permission of Faber and Faber. **135**

Horovitz, Frances, from 'In Painswick Churchyard', *Collected poems*, edited by Roger Garfitt. © Roger Garfitt and used with his kind permission. **136**

Mordaunt, Thomas Osbert. **135**

Shakespeare, William. **136**

Tagore, Rabindranath. Reproduced with permission of Macmillan General Books. **136**

Every endeavour has been made to trace the copyright owners of each extract. There do, however, remain a few extracts for which the source is unknown to the compiler and publisher. The publisher would be glad to hear from the copyright owners of these extracts and due acknowledgement will be made in all future editions of the book.